Molly's Veil

Molly's Veil

Sharon Bajer

Molly's Veil
first published 2005 by
Scirocco Drama
An imprint of J. Gordon Shillingford Publishing Inc.
© 2005 Sharon Bajer

Scirocco Drama Editor: Glenda MacFarlane
Cover design by Terry Gallagher/Doowah Design Inc.
Author photo by Nick Seiflow
Printed and bound in Canada

The photos of Margaret Grier (Powis, John, PA-126401) and Charlotte Whitton (Karsh, Yousuf, PA-206646) are reproduced with the permission of Library and Archives Canada.
"The Honeysuckle and the Bee" is from a Vaudeville musical entitled *Bluebell in Fairyland* (1901), written by Albert H. Fitz and composed by William H. Penn.

We acknowledge the financial support of the Manitoba Arts Council, The Canada Council for the Arts and the Government of Canada through the Book Publishing Industry Development Program (BPIDP) for our publishing program.

All rights reserved. No part of this book may be reproduced, for any reason, by any means, without the permission of the publisher. This play is fully protected under the copyright laws of Canada and all other countries of the Copyright Union and is subject to royalty. Changes to the text are expressly forbidden without written consent of the author. Rights to produce, film, record in whole or in part, in any medium or in any language, by any group amateur or professional, are retained by the author.
Production inquiries should be addressed to:
Playwrights Guild of Canada
54 Wolseley Street, 2nd Floor
Toronto, ON M5T 1A5
Phone 416-703-0201, FAX 416-703-0059
info@playwrightsguild.ca

Canadian Cataloguing in Publication Data

Bajer, Sharon, 1968-
    Molly's veil/Sharon Bajer.

A play.
ISBN 0-920486-80-0

    1. Whitton, Charlotte, 1896-1975—Drama. I. Title.

PS8306.A46M64 2005   C812'.6   C2005-901889-5

J. Gordon Shillingford Publishing
P.O. Box 86, RPO Corydon Avenue, Winnipeg, MB Canada R3M 3S3

for Carson

Playwright's Notes

I was first inspired to write a play about Charlotte Whitton after reading an article in *The National Post* entitled "Love Secrets of a Popular Politician." It spoke of a woman who was the first female mayor in Canada, whom I knew little about. Upon further investigation, I discovered that in addition to being the very outspoken, witty, and controversial mayor of Ottawa in the 1950s, she had been a pioneer in the development of Child Welfare in Canada and held an appointment with the League of Nations. She also had a secret box of letters that she bequeathed to the National Archives of Canada with instructions that it not be opened until 25 years after her death. What I found in that secret box was the world Ms. Whitton had kept out of the public eye—the world of Lottie and Mardie.

Prairie Theatre Exchange has been very supportive in the development of this play and I thank Cherry Karpishyn, Bob Metcalfe and all the staff and crew who have made my journey as a playwright possible. I also thank Allen McInnis and Brian Drader for their dramaturgical support and unwavering belief in the play. Thanks to the Manitoba Association of Playwrights, the Manitoba Arts Council, the Winnipeg Arts Council, On the Verge Festival, the Playwright's Atlantic Resource Centre, Library and Archives Canada and Theatre Projects for their ongoing support. Thanks to all the actors who participated in various workshops and readings of the play. Special thanks to the cast and design team of the PTE premiere and to my kids Ameena and George for being sweet and patient with me.

Production Information

Molly's Veil premiered on February 24, 2005 at Prairie Theatre Exchange, Winnipeg, Canada, with the following cast and crew:

CHARLOTTE	Maggie Nagle
MARGARET	Dawn Petten
BILL	Steven Ratzlaff
EMILY	Miriam Smith
PROFESSOR GORDON	Marina Stephenson Kerr

Director	Robert Metcalfe
Set and Costume Design	Carole Klemm
Lighting Design	Scott Henderson
Composer/Sound Designer	Don Benedictson
Stage Manager	Georgette Nairn
Assistant Stage Manager	Karyn Kumhyr

Characters

CHARLOTTE WHITTON

MARGARET GRIER

EMILY WICKS/PENELOPE/
WOMAN/MAN/VOICE 1

BILL KING/RADIO ANNOUNCER

PROFESSOR GORDON (MIN.)/ELIZABETH/
LORD MAYOR OF LONDON/VOICE 2/MAGISTRATE

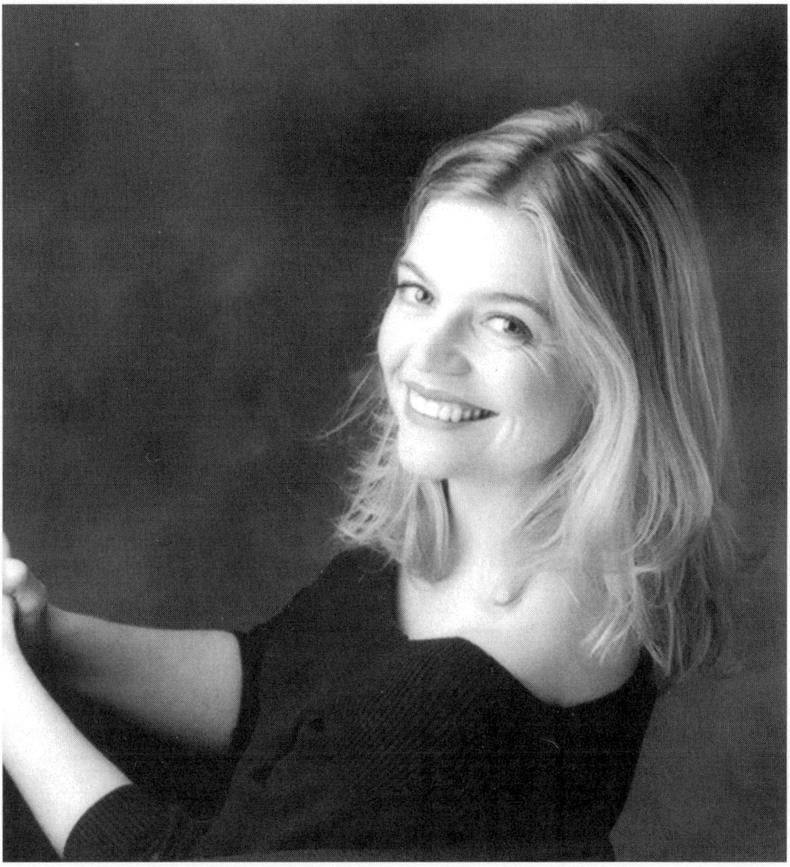

Sharon Bajer

Sharon Bajer is an actress, playwright, and director. She is the author of *Jesus Does Laundry Too, The Mother Load* and co-author of *The Apartment*. In 2002, Sharon was nominated for the John Hirsch Award for Most Promising Manitoba Writer.

Charlotte Whitton

Margaret Grier

Act I

A spotlight comes up on RADIO ANNOUNCER standing behind a microphone. The year is 1951. The place, Ottawa.

RADIO
ANNOUNCER: October 15th, 1951. A monumental event took place in Ottawa today as Canada's first lady mayor, Charlotte Elizabeth Hazeltyne Whitton was inaugurated in the Nation's Capital this afternoon. Miss Whitton has only been back in the political arena for two years, but the citizens of Ottawa are no strangers to the feisty five-foot fireball.

CHARLOTTE runs in followed by the ladies, sewing up the hem on her robes.

CHARLOTTE: For goodness sake, ladies, hurry it up! What are you doing down there, sewing a quilt?

RADIO
ANNOUNCER: Her all-female campaign committee, known as "The Thread and Needle Brigade" to signify that Ottawa's "pants needed patching" was a domestic analogy that dominated the race and it appears to have paid off. It was reported today that one of the first things Mayor Whitton did after taking up the municipal reins was to promptly get rid of the official limousine of office along with its chauffeur. When asked why she did this Miss Whitton replied—

CHARLOTTE: I've never had a man or a Cadillac in my life.

RADIO
ANNOUNCER: *(He laughs good naturedly.)* We will be hearing excerpts from that speech momentarily. Miss Whitton appears to have dusted off the official mayoral robes of office. We haven't seen those things in over a decade! The Thread and Needle Brigade must have had their work cut out for them—sewing up that ancient hem! *(He laughs "good naturedly".)*

CHARLOTTE: *(To ANNOUNCER.)* You think you're funny, do you? Well done, ladies. That will have to do. *(The ladies run off.)* Someone please fetch me my hat. *(To ANNOUNCER.)* Carry on then.

RADIO
ANNOUNCER: Thank you. Her meteoric rise with the Canadian Council on Child Welfare evoked extreme reactions as she championed the causes of single working girls, illegitimate children and unwed mothers. As did her admirable appointment to the League of Nations.

WOMAN: *(Enters.)* To have this woman on the League committee is absurd! Women need these honours as much as pigs need skates!

CHARLOTTE: Madam, every pig is better for a nice curly tail. Perhaps you could afford to focus your attention a little more at that end.

WOMAN: Oh! *(She exits.)*

RADIO
ANNOUNCER: Accused of being rude on many occasions, she's been known to shock even the most cultivated of men. Upon meeting the Lord Mayor of London—

LORD MAYOR: *(Enters wearing the chain of office.)* Ms. Whitton, how wonderful to meet you. I couldn't help but stare at the lovely adornment on your bosom and wondered if I smelled your rose, would you blush?

Sharon Bajer

CHARLOTTE: Lord Mayor, It is indeed a pleasure. I too had a query about that lovely decoration around your neck and wondered if I pulled your chain would you flush?

LORD MAYOR: I say! *(He exits.)*

RADIO
ANNOUNCER: Often referred to simply as—

MAN: *(Enters.)* That woman!

RADIO
ANNOUNCER: —she was known to inspire passionate debate.

MAN: Damn! Damn! Damn that woman!

CHARLOTTE: Mr. Chairman, may I remind you that I do have the floor. *(She pulls out a gun.)*

ALL: Ahhhhhhh! *(He runs off.)*

CHARLOTTE: It was only a toy!

RADIO
ANNOUNCER: *(CHARLOTTE begins a low, regal curtsey.)* Well, I think she's finally ready to begin her speech...no wait, she's doing something—bending...in what appears to be a low curtsey of some kind.

ELIZABETH
TUDOR: *(Enters.)* That's excellent, Charlotte.

CHARLOTTE: Your Majesty!

ELIZABETH: You must always face northeast when humbling yourself to England.

CHARLOTTE: Like this?

ELIZABETH: That's very nice. Straight back, bowed head. Lower, very slowly.

RADIO
ANNOUNCER: This is looking more and more like a coronation instead of an inauguration…

CHARLOTTE
& ELIZABETH: Oh pish tosh!

ELIZABETH: And don't take any guff! Remember…

CHARLOTTE: A woman has to work twice as hard as a man to be thought of half as good. Luckily, this is not difficult.

ELIZABETH: But you mustn't ever show them your weakness!

CHARLOTTE: I promise.

ELIZABETH: Carry on then!

ELIZABETH exits.

RADIO
ANNOUNCER: But in all seriousness, she appears ready to begin…

CHARLOTTE: Mr. Controllers and Aldermen, it would be unseemly not to preface this inauguration with a humble expression of our gratitude to almighty God that his Majesty, the King makes steady progress to health again. By your vote, you have entrusted me with the high honour of mayor of the city of Ottawa. As an unmarried woman, my mother and the friend with whom I shared my life both gone…

A woman stands up from the audience and calls to CHARLOTTE.

MARGARET: Charlotte!

CHARLOTTE: I promise to devote to this city all that I have within me…

MARGARET: Charlotte!

CHARLOTTE: *(Getting distracted by the calling.)* ...all that I have within me...

MARGARET: Charlotte!

CHARLOTTE: To give strength and devotion to her service...

MARGARET: Look at my little Lottie!

CHARLOTTE: *(Breaking out of her speech and addressing the woman.)* Margaret?

MARGARET: Charlotte, look at you!

CHARLOTTE: Margaret, do you see? I'm the mayor.

MARGARET: I see that. Congratulations! The hair is good. A bit mannish.

CHARLOTTE: It's modern. And less trouble in the wind. Do you like it?

MARGARET: The pomp suits you. You resemble a sea captain.

CHARLOTTE: Too much, do you think? Perhaps I should lose the hat.

MARGARET: No no, the hat is the best part. *(Laughs.)*

CHARLOTTE: I'm glad you like it.

MARGARET: Oh, yes.

Pause.

CHARLOTTE: I wasn't expecting you today, Margaret.

MARGARET: You know I would never miss one of your speeches.

CHARLOTTE: I really can't talk to you right now.

Pause.

MARGARET: I just wanted to give you something. *(She hands her a very heavy wrapped present.)* To decorate your new office with, Madame Mayor.

CHARLOTTE: *(Takes the present and excitedly tears off the paper like a little girl on her birthday.)* For me? Oh Margaret! I wasn't expecting… you always give the most thoughtful presents. Oh what can it be? It's so heavy? What can it possibly be?

MARGARET: Well, I suppose you'll just have to open it and see.

> *Charlotte slowly lifts out the plaster bust of a woman. It is Queen Elizabeth I.*

CHARLOTTE: Ohhhh. Elizabeth!

MARGARET: For inspiration.

CHARLOTTE: This was mine! From when I was just a child. Wherever did you find her?

MARGARET: I thought it was time the two of you were reunited.

CHARLOTTE: Thank you.

MARGARET: You've worked hard for it. It's a great tribute to become a mayor—the people really love you.

CHARLOTTE: Yes. It's good to see you Margaret, but I'm afraid I can't let you stay long.

MARGARET: No?

CHARLOTTE: You know I can't.

MARGARET: Well, Elizabeth can stay. *(She turns to go and stops.)* Oh, I nearly forgot! Look inside.

> *CHARLOTTE turns the bust over and takes out a book that has been placed inside.*

CHARLOTTE: Margaret! You know I can't keep this here! Put it back where you found it at once!

> *A young woman enters.*

EMILY: Excuse me, Mayor Whitton?

CHARLOTTE: Ahhh!

EMILY: Oh, sorry! I didn't mean...I thought you were talking to someone.

CHARLOTTE: *(Hiding the book.)* Oh, no, I wasn't.

MARGARET: Aren't I someone?

Pause.

CHARLOTTE: Is the ceremony over?

EMILY: Why, of course.

CHARLOTTE: Was I good?

EMILY: Oh, Mayor Whitton, you gave a marvelous speech, as usual. So inspired and—

MARGARET: I want to see your new office!

CHARLOTTE: Do you want to see my new office?

EMILY: Right now?

MARGARET: Oh yes!

CHARLOTTE: Why not? Come with me.

MARGARET enters the office first, the doors opening magically, then CHARLOTTE enters, using her key.

MARGARET: Oooo. Isn't it fancy?

CHARLOTTE: Very impressive.

EMILY: Yes.

CHARLOTTE: We're going to need a few things changed.

MARGARET: A coat rack for one.

CHARLOTTE: Have you a name, dear?

EMILY: Oh, your worship, hasn't anyone—

CHARLOTTE
& MARGARET: Your worship?

CHARLOTTE: Did you just call me *your worship*?

EMILY: Isn't that what I'm supposed to call you?

CHARLOTTE: Good heavens! Flattering though that may be, I won't have it. You will call me Charlotte.

EMILY: Swell. And my name is Emily. Emily Wicks.

MARGARET: And I'm Margaret.

Pause.

CHARLOTTE: Well Miss Emily Wicks, the first thing we must do is get this confounded typewriter out of here. I can't stand the bloody things!

EMILY: *(Still with the coat, goes to pick up the typewriter which is very heavy.)* Righto.

CHARLOTTE: Oh! I didn't mean for *you* to lift the blasted thing. The building is filled to the rafters with the *other* species. We'll get one of those puffed up men to do it—they must be good for something.

EMILY: Oh, that's funny! Do you mind if I write that down?

CHARLOTTE: No of course not, why should I? And now, the big moment! Drum roll, please!

MARGARET: Certainly Madam.

She starts a drum roll on the side of the desk.

EMILY: Um… okay, I'll try. *(She attempts to make the sound of a drum roll with her mouth.)* Bum, bum…bum, bum….bum.

> CHARLOTTE *finally sits at her new desk with a great flourish and she looks ridiculously small.* EMILY *suppresses her laughter.*

CHARLOTTE: Miss Wicks, surely you are not here merely to follow me around, because if you are, we really must send out for elocution lessons immediately.

EMILY: Oh no. I'm a journalist.

MARGARET: A journalist!

CHARLOTTE: Oh well!

MARGARET: How wonderful.

CHARLOTTE: Who with?

EMILY: *Time* magazine.

CHARLOTTE: *Time*!

MARGARET: Oh dear.

CHARLOTTE: A reporter!

EMILY: Oh, I'm not a reporter, I'm a journalist.

CHARLOTTE: Well there's nothing to report here, so I suggest you be on your way.

EMILY: I'm not a reporter. I'm doing a profile on you.

MARGARET: A profile! How exciting!

CHARLOTTE: Well, someone could have told me about it. I'm sorry, but the last time I ended up in your magazine, it was for something I'd really rather put behind me.

EMILY: Oh…but it's all arranged! I have a photographer coming Monday.

CHARLOTTE: On my first day of work!?

EMILY: That was my idea. I thought if I could just watch, follow you around—I promise you, I'm crazy keen.

CHARLOTTE: Apparently.

EMILY: I've been an admirer of yours for years.

MARGARET: An admirer!

EMILY: I had to really fight with them to be allowed to do it at all.

CHARLOTTE: I have a big day come Monday.

EMILY: Of course.

CHARLOTTE: One of my first assignments is to welcome Princess Elizabeth and Prince Phillip on their official tour of Ottawa and I can't for the life of me decide what to wear.

MARGARET: Oh, I know! How about—

CHARLOTTE: I mustn't have any distraction!

MARGARET: Sorry, luv.

EMILY: Listen, I know a thing or two about fashion. I could help you!

CHARLOTTE: Miss Wicks. I am refusing to grant you an interview—

MARGARET: Profile.

EMILY: Profile.

CHARLOTTE: Pardon me?

EMILY: Profile, it's a…profile. Much more than an interview, they want to put your face on the cover. As…um…Man of the Year.

MARGARET: *(Gasps.)*

Pause.

CHARLOTTE: Get your pen.

EMILY: Really? Oh, thank you, Miss Whitton. I promise you, It'll really razz your berries!

CHARLOTTE: It will what?

EMILY: You'll like it. I'm gonna show you in a great light. You can trust me. I need to run back to the hotel and get my things. It's just across the street.

CHARLOTTE: Fine.

EMILY: Holy cow, this is going to be just swell! *(She exits.)*

MARGARET: Holy cow. What does that mean?

CHARLOTTE: Oh dear.

MARGARET: I hope she can write better than she speaks.

CHARLOTTE: That would be the hope.

MARGARET: You really must have them get you a taller chair, luv.

CHARLOTTE: Margaret—

MARGARET: Or a smaller desk.

CHARLOTTE: Margaret, you really shouldn't be here.

MARGARET: I couldn't very well miss your big day.

CHARLOTTE: I know, luv, but it's going to be different now that I'm the mayor. I thought I had been quite clear in my last letter to you.

MARGARET: There have been so many last letters, Charlotte. I can never be sure if it's really the last one or not.

CHARLOTTE: Yes—that's my fault, but...Margaret, about the book...

MARGARET: I thought you might want to have it here, that's all. I can get rid of it if you don't want it anymore.

CHARLOTTE: No! I do want it.

MARGARET: Or *you* could get rid of it rather.

CHARLOTTE: I don't want to get rid of it.

MARGARET: If it embarrasses you—

CHARLOTTE: Of course it doesn't!

MARGARET: Even if it were between the pages of *Time* magazine? *(She hands the book to CHARLOTTE.)*

CHARLOTTE: Margaret, you know that's impossible.

MARGARET: Is it?

Pause.

CHARLOTTE: Oh, let's just have one toast and then you'll be off.

MARGARET: We have nothing to toast with.

CHARLOTTE: They've got to have liquor hidden here somewhere. Man cannot live by incompetence alone! *(She goes rifling through the desk.)*

MARGARET: You're not going to find any booze in there, Charlotte. This is city hall.

CHARLOTTE: *(Emerging triumphant with a bottle and two glasses.)* Eureka!

MARGARET: The devils.

CHARLOTTE: *(Pouring.)* Why don't *you* give it.

MARGARET: No, I hate to. You know I can't give speeches. I have to have it all planned out—what I'm going to say first.

CHARLOTTE: You're exaggerating.

MARGARET: I'm not! Don't you remember how shy I was at university? I absolutely dreaded being called up to speak. And somehow Professor Min always singled me out.

CHARLOTTE: Professor Min. My, how that woman could give a toast!

MARGARET: She never liked me.

CHARLOTTE: Margaret!

PROFESSOR WILHEMINA GORDON enters with a glass and holds it up in a toast. Queen's University, 1916.

MIN: Gather around, girls!

The sound of an old gramophone is heard. PENELOPE runs on with a table and MARGARET and CHARLOTTE take their drinks and gather around it.

MIN: Firstly, I would like to thank you for the generous invitation to dine with you tonight. It looks as though someone went to a great deal of effort in arranging this beautiful table and I can't help but wonder when they found time to study.

The girls laugh.

I would like to propose a toast to the women of the Levana Society. You girls have unceasingly supported the war effort and have added to the Queen's spirit of which we have been so proud.

The girls cheer.

I don't know if you realize that this year, 1916 breaks a significant record for us. Women now make up 68 percent of this university's population!

The girls cheer.

It is a shame that the path of opportunity for us is laid at the expense of our boys now fighting overseas, but I believe this nation will be stronger for it.

The girls agree.

The Roman Goddess, Levana, binds us with the wonder women of old days. Levana, raising the human infant in her hands is a reminder to us that the body is bound to the mind. Now, let's eat heartily, girls.

Biggest cheer of all. Clinking of glasses.

MIN: Thank you for that. I encourage spontaneous toasting as you all know. Now pass the peas, dear heart.

CHARLOTTE: Who has the peas? Penelope?

PENELOPE: Mardie, pass the peas down to Charlotte. Martin! Margaret! The peas dear.

MARGARET: Oh yes, roast beef?

MIN: Yes, please, and the peas.

MARGARET: Here you are, Professor.

MIN: Chin chin.

PENELOPE: Where are you, Margie?

CHARLOTTE: Where indeed?

MARGARET: Sorry?

PENELOPE: Dreaming.

MARGARET: Oh, yes, sorry. I was thinking. About the boys. Salt, please.

CHARLOTTE: Here you are, laddie.

MARGARET: Thank you luv.

MIN:	Yes it's hard not to wonder what they're eating tonight. Over there, you know.
PENELOPE:	Potatoes, sport?
CHARLOTTE:	Yes, please, Penelope.
MARGARET:	You know, so many of those boys went off to fight—barely able to even lift a rifle. Many of them would have been studying at this very university. I feel so fortunate to be here at Queens with all of you, but I do feel conflicted, benefiting at their expense.
MIN:	How many men have benefited at the expense of women do you think?
CHARLOTTE:	You know the saying…
PENELOPE:	Behind every great man…
ALL:	There is an even greater woman.
CHARLOTTE:	Who is no doubt wondering why her husband receives all the glory.
PENELOPE:	Charlotte, I very much enjoyed your article in *The Queen's Journal*, by the way.
MIN:	Oh yes, it was a marvelous parody.
PENELOPE:	Imagine, a woman for Prime Minister. It's not so far-fetched!
MIN:	Mmm, is that fennel I'm tasting?
PENELOPE:	Oh oh oh, girls! We have a winner of tonight's mystery herb contest!
MIN:	Oh, thank you, old chap!
PENELOPE:	Wait till you see the prize!
MIN:	My word. May I have the buns?

CHARLOTTE: *(Standing to give a spontaneous toast.)* Never in any land has the need for intelligent womanhood been so great as in the Dominion of Canada today!

ALL: Hear, hear!

PENELOPE: And never has the opportunity for women's service been as wide and glorious!

ALL: Cheers! Bravo! Chin chin!

> *They all look to MARGARET expecting her to toast next.*

MIN: Your turn now, Margaret.

MARGARET: I really don't know what to say.

CHARLOTTE: It doesn't have to be fancy. Just anything! Whatever comes into your head first!

> *MARGARET stands with her glass held up trying to think of something fantastic to say.*

MARGARET: Cheers. I hope the roast isn't too dry. If it is, then...I think I may cry.

MIN: A rhyme, how...clever.

PENELOPE: Min, why don't you do another? Inspire us!

MIN: *(Standing and raising her glass.)* To your careers you must give all or not at all!

All: Absolutely. Amen.

MIN: There will be times when you will all feel that your paths are uncharted. Your friends will marry and the pressure to bear children will weigh heavily on your souls. But always remember; in times of loneliness there lies a great strength. Your choice becomes whether to access it and use it or press it down. If you choose the latter, be prepared to face your worst enemy—your unfulfilled self. *(Pause.)*

Sharon Bajer

And speaking of one's unfulfilled self, who emptied the gravy boat? *(Laughter.)*

MARGARET: I confess...

PENELOPE: Martin, you can't give a speech, but you do enjoy your gravy. Pass it here, luv, there's plenty more when that came from. *(She exits with the gravy boat.)*

CHARLOTTE: No, Min put it just right...our task in the outside world is to think and act independently of social pressure.

MARGARET: It is burdensome though, isn't it? Sheep are such well cared for creatures—you find yourself lost among them. And what really lies beyond the fence? Perhaps the wolf will eat you.

MIN: What are you going on about, Mardie?

MARGARET: Oh, I don't know. I don't often venture with my tongue.

CHARLOTTE: That was inspired! You're a poet!

MIN: A poetess. Give us one then.

MARGARET: A what?

MIN: A poem.

CHARLOTTE: Yes, do!

MARGARET: No, no. I couldn't.

CHARLOTTE: Just a little one.

MARGARET: Oh, later maybe. I've lost my train of thought.

MIN: Well, while you are composing, I'm going to go and see what's become of that gravy. A woman can't be trusted alone with the drippings. Excuse me.

She exits.

MARGARET: I'm afraid the professor really doesn't think much of me.

CHARLOTTE: Nonsense, she's just trying to push you a bit. It's her way. She'll warm to you if you show her that you're not afraid of her.

MARGARET: She terrifies me!

CHARLOTTE: Then we have our work cut out for us, don't we? I'll help you.

MARGARET: Thank you, Charl. Now about this linen arrangement. Who *was* responsible for putting these wretched combinations together?

CHARLOTTE: *(Feigning innocence.)* I haven't the foggiest.

MARGARET: Oh Charles, I'm glad to see that you don't know how to do everything.

> *CHARLOTTE and MARGARET share a smile. Min takes the table off.*
>
> *There is a knock on the door which breaks this memory. EMILY enters.*

EMILY: All settled in I see. The commissioner gave me a bit of a hard time. I didn't think he was going to let me pass, but then I remembered my press card. I keep forgetting that I have it because I never had to use it before. Not that I haven't covered important events, but I'm usually with the photographer and he's a man so they usually don't make such a big deal. You know what I mean? Is there a good place that I can sit do you think?

CHARLOTTE: I can think of one or two places.

MARGARET: Be nice.

CHARLOTTE: You may sit right there. *(She gestures to the chair in which MARGARET is sitting.)*

EMILY: That's swell. (*MARGARET vacates the chair just as EMILY sits. EMILY notices the two glasses.*) Oh. Is this meant for me?

CHARLOTTE: Indeed.

EMILY: Gee, I hardly ever touch liquor.

CHARLOTTE: Live a little.

EMILY: I guess on such an exciting day it wouldn't hurt to have a little drop. (*She takes a tentative sip, makes a sour face and then drinks it all.*) Oh, yum.

MARGARET: (*As CHARLOTTE pours EMILY another glass.*) You're going to get the poor girl drunk.

CHARLOTTE: Just help yourself to the bottle Miss Wicks. You seem very young to be working for *Time* magazine are you not?

EMILY: Oh no, I'm not young at all! I'm twenty eight—

CHARLOTTE: Very persistent then—

EMILY: I like to think it's because I'm a good journalist—

CHARLOTTE: You're not married or engaged or any of that nonsense I hope—

EMILY: Miss Whitton I thought I was supposed to be interviewing *you*.

MARGARET: Charlotte, let the girl talk for goodness sake.

CHARLOTTE: You're right. Where did you attend college?

EMILY: Queen's. Same as you.

MARGARET: A sister!

CHARLOTTE: You should have said something earlier.

EMILY: I went to lots of your guest lectures—every one I think. In fact, you're the reason that I stuck it out through college. You could say that I owe my journalism degree to you!

CHARLOTTE: Absolutely not! You must relish your own achievements. They are, after all the only things that remain with you in the end.

MARGARET: Is that right?

EMILY: Yes, I've heard you say that many times. There are lots of your expressions that I live by, including your vow of celibacy.

MARGARET: Your what?

CHARLOTTE: My what?

EMILY: You've always said to choose between a husband, or a job and not try to have both. Well, I've really stuck by your words.

MARGARET: Oh dear.

EMILY: Sorry, we've gone right off topic, haven't we?

MARGARET: She's very idealistic, this one. You might want to set the poor girl straight before she ends up living her whole life as a nun.

CHARLOTTE: Where do we begin?

EMILY: *(Referring to her notes.)* I thought we could start with some questions about your work with the Canadian Council on Child Welfare. You started there in 1920, right?

CHARLOTTE: Yes.

EMILY: That must have been really neat—

CHARLOTTE: "Neat." Yes, it really "razzed my berries," in fact.

MARGARET: Be nice!

CHARLOTTE: You know, I started off as a journalist of sorts. In a

	way that's how I ended up with the Council. You should consider your position very fortunate. There were not a lot of interesting careers for women in 1918, I can tell you.
EMILY:	That's when you graduated?
CHARLOTTE:	Yes.
EMILY:	I didn't know you were a writer.
CHARLOTTE:	Oh yes.
MARGARET:	Why don't you show her your book?
CHARLOTTE:	My book?
EMILY:	You're writing a book?
MARGARET:	A make-believe.
CHARLOTTE:	Not now.
EMILY:	No, of course not now, I should think that you have your hands full at the moment.
CHARLOTTE:	Oh yes. Very.
EMILY:	If you don't mind, I'd like to hear more about your time at Queen's. Was it all study, or did you have other interests as well. A sweetheart, maybe?
MARGARET:	Oh this should be good.
CHARLOTTE:	I had a number of interests. Everyone seemed sweet in those days. There was a sense of decorum that seems to have gone by the wayside now. People treated each other with respect. And men and women were so polite and careful with each other.
MARGARET:	What are you talking about?
CHARLOTTE:	Courtship rituals.

EMILY: Tell me about those.

MARGARET: Yes, I'd love to hear them.

>*BILL KING enters. Queen's University, 1918.*

BILL: Excuse me, Miss?

CHARLOTTE: *Miss?*

MARGARET: Oh no, wait. You were just coming back from practice. You have to have your stick.

>*She hands CHARLOTTE a field hockey stick.*

CHARLOTTE: Oh yes, very important. Thank you.

MARGARET: My pleasure. Carry on.

BILL: Excuse me, Miss?

CHARLOTTE: Miss?

BILL: Ma'am, uh…I'm sorry, I didn't mean to put you off—it's so hard to know what's correct nowadays.

CHARLOTTE: Try again.

BILL: Dear…lady.

CHARLOTTE: Whatever my sex, I'm no lady!

BILL: Yes sir!

CHARLOTTE: And you are?

BILL: The name's Bill. Bill King.

CHARLOTTE: King. Interesting name. I'm Charlotte…but my friends call me Lottie or Charl or Charles or Sharlie…

BILL: I think I'll stick to Charlotte to stay on the safe side.

CHARLOTTE: Good call.

BILL: Actually, I do know who you are, I just wasn't sure it was you... I mean, you are the Charlotte Whitton that writes for the *Queen's Journal*?

CHARLOTTE: I certainly hope so.

BILL: You play a mean game of field hockey.

CHARLOTTE: Are you looking to challenge me to a game, Mr. King?

BILL: Well...the idea hadn't occurred to me, but now that you suggest it, yes, that would be outstanding! Ha ha. No...I actually wanted to talk to you about your article in last month's issue.

CHARLOTTE: That certainly stirred up the honey pot.

BILL: Um...don't you mean the bee's nest?

CHARLOTTE: In my analogy the bees are eating.

BILL: Honey.

CHARLOTTE: Exactly.

BILL: Because they're what...hungry?

CHARLOTTE: Narcissistic.

BILL: Narcissistic bees.

CHARLOTTE: Yes.

Pause.

BILL: *(He pulls out the article from his pocket.)* I just wanted to ask you...I have the article right here...in this section you say, "...because we succeed, we are satisfied and happy. —And therefore circumscribed by the narrowness of our desires..." Do you really believe that? I mean, here you are, studying at a university—surely you want to succeed—isn't that why we're all here? To succeed, to make a life for ourselves, to attain happiness? Maybe that's why people get married, to help each other reach those ideals. That would be called success in my book.

CHARLOTTE: "By all means marry; if you get a good wife, you'll be happy. If you get a bad one, you'll become a philosopher." That's Socrates, in case you're wondering.

BILL: Don't you want to be happy? We all want to be happy. I don't think Socrates was.

CHARLOTTE: Were that grand thinker to emerge on this campus today, he would become an inmate of practicalities in a fortnight and Demosthenes arrested for vagrancy on the sea shore.

BILL: I'm not great on those darn Greeks. Demosthenes was the stutterer wasn't he? Sucked on pebbles. I better get myself a bad wife so that I can keep up with you.

CHARLOTTE: Demosthenes didn't "suck on pebbles" as you say. He kept them in his mouth so that he could overcome his speech impediment. And he became one of the greatest orators of his time. He knew how to work hard to overcome adversity. His desires were huge! Oh how I long for the good old days!

BILL: I'm sorry to disappoint you, but these *are* the good old days.

CHARLOTTE: No, no—I mean 400 B.C. or thereabouts.

BILL: 400 B.C.?

CHARLOTTE: Or thereabouts.

BILL: I can picture you quite nicely in a toga actually.

CHARLOTTE: *(Smacking his arm.)* Be quiet, I'm quoting. Listen and you may learn something. "The greatest way to live with honour is to be what you pretend to be."

BILL: Hm. That's pretty good. I must apply that in regard to my current fascination. By the way, you dropped this.

He hands her a ball.

CHARLOTTE: Oh.

BILL: "Get not your friends by bare compliments, but by giving them sensible tokens of your love."

CHARLOTTE: Liar. You do know your Greeks.

Pause.

CHARLOTTE: What's your field of study Mr. King?

BILL: Journalism actually. Very practical. Very bee-like. *(He buzzes.)*

CHARLOTTE: You know of course, that in the bee colony, even Kings must answer to the Queen.

BILL: Perhaps that's the attraction.

PROFESSOR GORDON enters.

MIN: It's wonderful to see two of my star students hanging about together.

BILL: Professor Gordon!

CHARLOTTE: We've only just met actually. I'd hardly consider that hanging about together.

BILL: You were right, Professor. Miss Whitton has disagreed with absolutely everything I said.

CHARLOTTE: That's not true.

BILL: You see?

MIN: I knew you'd hit it off.

CHARLOTTE: Min, I was hoping I could meet with you later today about my essay on child labour.

MIN: I'm afraid I have no extra time today, but you know, Bill is something of an expert on the subject, aren't you Bill.

BILL: Am I? Yes—I certainly…believe it to be true!

CHARLOTTE: Humph.

MIN: Why don't the two of you write something together—for the next issue of the *Queen's Journal* perhaps?

CHARLOTTE: Oh no, I don't think—

BILL: What a splendid idea!

MIN: It would be good for you, Charlotte, to learn how to collaborate with other people.

CHARLOTTE: I really don't believe—

MIN: I'm afraid I must insist.

BILL: She insists. That means we have no choice.

CHARLOTTE: I know what it means.

MIN: This is wonderful! Sometimes opposing points of view can make for a very interesting partnership. You both might discover things you never thought you knew. Consider it an assignment.

She exits.

BILL: I'm available to meet later for tea. We could get started right away if you like.

CHARLOTTE: Very well.

BILL: The campus lounge at four o'clock. Suits you?

CHARLOTTE: Fine.

BILL: Chippy. I'll try not to use up all the honey.

CHARLOTTE: And I'll try not to sting. *(He exits and CHARLOTTE crosses back to her desk.)* Chippy! Chippy! I could have hit him with my stick!

MARGARET: He liked you. I don't blame him. You're very charming when you're angry.

EMILY: Oh dear. Turbulent!

CHARLOTTE: *(To MARGARET.)* Enough out of you—

EMILY: Sorry. I'll try not to interrupt. But, dare I ask—how did the article turn out?

CHARLOTTE: It was bloody good! So good in fact that later the next year, both Mr. King and I were hand chosen as "keen young graduates" to come and work for the Social Service Council of Canada.

EMILY: That's when you came to Ottawa?

CHARLOTTE: No, the organization was in Toronto at the time.

EMILY: It must have been nice to have Mr. King there with you…

CHARLOTTE: Oh, Mr. King declined the offer. He felt his duty was elsewhere.

MARGARET: He did that for you, you know.

EMILY: So, after school was over, you had to leave your friends and your sweetheart?

CHARLOTTE: That's what happens when things come to an end. You all must follow your heart's desire.

MARGARET: Your heart's what?

EMILY: Your heart's desire. That's nice. Listen, thanks for being so honest with me about your personal life.

It's going to make the profile so much more… personal.

CHARLOTTE: You really do have a way with words, Miss Wicks.

EMILY: *(Referring to herself.)* Journalist.

MARGARET: And you have a severe case of selective memory. You should really tell her the truth. *(She starts humming a tune.)*

CHARLOTTE: That song—what is it? You used to hum it.

EMILY: I did?

MARGARET: It's easy to remember the taste of jam or the smell of the wind from the river, or a song from your childhood— *(Humming.)*

CHARLOTTE: Oh, don't be a poetess! Just tell me the name of the damn thing.

EMILY: I don't hear any music.

MARGARET: —but the words to the melody are more elusive— one often selects what they'd like the words to have been instead of what they actually were. *(Humming.)*

EMILY: Maybe it's outside.

CHARLOTTE: Yes! Yes it's outside. Why don't you go and have a look.

EMILY: You want me to look for…a tune?

CHARLOTTE: Yes, yes and hurry before it stops. Bring it back. I have to know the name of it.

EMILY: Oh…all right. Um…

CHARLOTTE: And don't come back until you have it.

EMILY: Until I have the song?

CHARLOTTE: Yes.

EMILY: *(Sighs.)* Only for you, Miss. Whitton. (*She exits.*)

CHARLOTTE: I've got it! It's on the tip of my...

> *MARGARET has set out a picnic basket and blanket on a hill overlooking the Ottawa River. 1918.*

Our hill! Oh look Margaret! We used to come up here all the time. I'd forgotten! Oh! Look how windy the river looks from way up here! Remember this place? Margaret? Oh, for pity's sake, Mardie, what *is* that tune?

MARGARET: I don't know. I've known it ever since I was a girl. It just comes to me now and again. I'll teach it to you before school's end, I promise.

CHARLOTTE: What a glorious day. I can't imagine any place I'd rather be.

MARGARET: Me too.

> *MIN enters breathing heavily.*

CHARLOTTE: Professor! You made it!

MIN: Who picked this spot?

CHARLOTTE & MARGARET: She did.

MIN: Well, it is rather out of the way. Poor Penelope is far too overdressed. I lost her on the hill somewhere.

CHARLOTTE: She'll be along. Margaret and I come up here almost daily. There's a wonderful view, see?

MIN: The only view I'm interested in at the moment is the inside of that picnic basket.

MARGARET: *(Bells.)* Listen to the church bells.

CHARLOTTE: It must be a wedding.

MIN: I'll have an egg, please.

MARGARET: *(Handing her an egg.)* But who would anyone be marrying? The men are all at war.

MIN: Most of the men are at war. There are some that refuse to go. Did someone remember to bring the napkins?

MARGARET: Penelope must have them.

MIN: I hope she's all right. Why don't you go and find her, Margaret?

MARGARET: Me?

MIN: It was your idea to come up here.

CHARLOTTE: No, you sit, I'll find her.

MIN: Just let Margaret do it, for heaven's sake.

CHARLOTTE: Oh, never mind, I think I see her coming now.

PENELOPE enters and collapses.

CHARLOTTE: Oh, Penelope. Thank God!

MARGARET: You've arrived. Well done!

PENELOPE: I've dressed too warmly I think.

MARGARET: Well just sit down and take off some of those things. It's no wonder you're hot.

PENELOPE: I'm all sweaty.

CHARLOTTE: Have some water.

PENELOPE: Oh thank you, dear heart.

MARGARET: Jam anyone?

PENELOPE: Oh!

MIN: Jam!

CHARLOTTE: Yes, thank you—wherever did you get jam?

MARGARET: I saved it for a special time.

CHARLOTTE: Margaret, you have the grace of a lioness.

PENELOPE: I'll open it.

MIN: Save some for the rest of us now.

PENELOPE: It is a nice view from here, isn't it?

MIN: I've got a picture exactly like it hanging in my office. And I don't have to hike for an hour to have a look at it. *(She swats a bug.)*

PENELOPE: Well, I think this is just heavenly. It's days like these that we'll remember for the rest of our lives I think.

CHARLOTTE: Margaret?

MARGARET: Yes?

CHARLOTTE: What do you plan to do when school is over?

MARGARET: I haven't given it much thought really. I don't have big ambitions like the rest of you.

CHARLOTTE: You're not thinking of marrying *yourself* are you?

MARGARET: Old Lott! If one could marry *oneself*, perhaps I would.

They laugh.

MARGARET: I really don't know what the future holds for me. I'm afraid I don't actually want a family or a career.

CHARLOTTE: What do you want?

MIN: I'd like the bread.

MARGARET: I'd like a little place in the country. A garden. Some place outside of the city, but close enough to a town so I could easily fetch supplies when I need them.

Molly's Veil

MIN: Those little towns are filled with lunatics. And inbred kittens.

MARGARET: Perhaps a little dog for company. I don't know. What I want to do and what I'm expected to do are so opposed. I don't want to feel as if I've wasted my education.

MIN: Education is never a waste.

CHARLOTTE: Besides, if you hadn't followed your path here, we would never have met.

MARGARET: Yes, I guess that's true.

CHARLOTTE: I've liked rooming with you these past two years. We must always keep in touch, even when we leave Queens.

MARGARET: Oh Charl. I would like that. *(Pause.)* I have something to give you all.

PENELOPE: Oh do!

CHARLOTTE: Yes!

MIN: A speech?

MARGARET: No it's not a speech. It's kind of well…a poem I suppose. I wrote it a while ago after we were reading Yeats.

PENELOPE: A poem! Fantastic!

MARGARET: It's nothing like Yeats—it's a silly poem.

CHARLOTTE: Oh read it!

PENELOPE: Read it to us!

MARGARET: Oh I can't. You read it, Charlotte. It's silly, I shouldn't have mentioned it.

CHARLOTTE: Too late!

MIN: We have you trapped.

PENELOPE: You must read it.

MARGARET: No no you've all made too much out of it already! You'll only be disappointed.

CHARLOTTE: Go on.

MIN: Where is it?

PENELOPE: Do you have it here?

MARGARET: No.

CHARLOTTE: She does!

MARGARET: Okay. Okay. I'll read it.

> *She pulls out a little drum and CHARLOTTE beats a rhythm to the poem. They've practiced this.*

The Ladies of Levana

The ladies of Levana house
Fear no man yet shriek at mouse
March they in to every fray
Strong, united, bold and gay
Pussy willows purr with glee
Lilies shake their dewy leaves
When lovely Levana ladies stride
The toast of Queen's and Kingston's pride!

MARGARET: That's it, what do you think?

PENELOPE: Brava!

CHARLOTTE: Wonderful, Margaret!

MIN: I didn't realize that you had such hidden talents!

MARGARET: Is it really all right?

PENELOPE: Margaret, it's fantastic—and so catchy!

MIN: I think you may have just replaced our University's anthem.

PENELOPE: I want to go swimming! There's a small lake up here, isn't there?

CHARLOTTE: Lake Little Bear. It's just there, maybe five hundred yards.

MARGARET: Very secluded. We swim there all the time.

CHARLOTTE: You don't even need your suits!

PENELOPE: Naturally! *(She starts taking off her clothes.)* Who's game?

MIN: Oh, what the heck. *(She also starts taking off her clothes.)*

CHARLOTTE: I really should digest first.

MARGARET: You two go on ahead. We'll catch up.

PENELOPE: Whistle if you see anyone coming!

CHARLOTTE: I don't know how to whistle. Do you?

MARGARET: I'm afraid not. What if we just bang on the drum?

PENELOPE: Oh, good idea.

MIN: I haven't done this in years. Heavens! If anyone sees me—hee hee. Last one in the water has to carry everything back down the hill! *(She runs off.)*

PENELOPE: Wait! That's not fair. Come on, you two! *(She runs off.)*

CHARLOTTE: That went very well, I think. You see?

MARGARET: It really did feel good! I don't know why I was so scared! Oh, Charlotte—you make me do the craziest things! I love it!

(She starts taking off her clothes.) Oh, I have a knot.

Help me with this.

> *CHARLOTTE gets up and helps her with her skirt. They start undressing each other as if this is the most natural thing in the world.*

CHARLOTTE: I really don't know how you're going to get on without me when school's done.

MARGARET: I've elected not to think about it. Let's just have fun today.

CHARLOTTE: I worry about you, Miss. Who's going to undo your knots—or get your sleepy head out of bed in the mornings?

MARGARET: Never mind that. Who's going to make sure you don't leave the house in dreadful combinations! Or a curl sticking up all the wrong way.

CHARLOTTE: I suppose we'll be lost. *(They are both standing there in their underwear.)*

MARGARET: Mhmm.

CHARLOTTE: You have a bit of jam here.

> *She reaches over and slowly wipes the jam off MARGARET's lip. MARGARET touches CHARLOTTE's hair. They remain locked in each other's gaze.*

BILL's VOICE: *(From off.)* Professor? Charlotte?

CHARLOTTE: Bill?

MARGARET: Oh my God!

CHARLOTTE: How did he get up here?

BILL: Where are you women?

MARGARET: Cover up!

CHARLOTTE: Hand me my skirt!

Molly's Veil

BILL: Penelope?

MARGARET: Here.

BILL: Are you girls up here?

MARGARET: What should I do?

CHARLOTTE: Take the clothes—go get dressed! I'll try and hold him off.

> *MARGARET runs around gathering the clothes and they frantically try and put their clothes back on. BILL continues to call. They giggle and get all tangled up etc. MARGARET runs off just as BILL enters.*

BILL: So this is your hideout!

CHARLOTTE: Bill! What are you doing up here? *(She picks up the drum and starts banging on it.)* I didn't know you were a hiker.

BILL: And I didn't know you were a musi...interested in music.

CHARLOTTE: I've only just started.

BILL: Very nice tune.

CHARLOTTE: What's that?

BILL: I said. Very...nice... *(She stops.)* tune!

CHARLOTTE: Thank you. It's called..."The Naughty Little Beaver."

BILL: Does it have any words?

CHARLOTTE: Why...yes it does.

BILL: Could you...sing a bit for me?

CHARLOTTE: *(Banging the drum as if smacking someone's bottom. She makes up the words as she plays.)*

> Naughty little bea-ver.
> Naughty little one.
> Chewing all the trees down.
> Isn't very…fun.
> For the…little….Fish-ies
> Swim-ming up the ri-ver.

MARGARET: *(Entering.)* Well those squirrels ran away just as soon as I got near! And I was only trying to feed them. Oh. Hello Bill.

BILL: Margaret.

MARGARET: Have you come for the concert?

BILL: The what?

CHARLOTTE: The concert. We ladies have formed a small orchestra and we're having a concert this very afternoon! You're welcome to join us if you like.

BILL: If I like? Well, no thank you. Although I'm sure it is…not to be missed. I was just looking for the professor, but I suppose if she's practicing I won't bother her. You're very good though. Do…keep it up. I…just wanted to give her a message. Perhaps you could do it for me.

CHARLOTTE: Of course, what's the message?

BILL: I've decided to enlist.

MARGARET: Enlist?!

CHARLOTTE: What on earth for?

BILL: They need me for training right away and I wanted to ask her if I could write my final examinations earlier. If you could just let her know.

MARGARET: Bill. It's crazy. You don't have to do this.

BILL: I wouldn't be much of a man if I continue to stand by and do nothing. It's my responsibility to go.

MARGARET: Charlotte, say something. Talk him out of it!

CHARLOTTE: I'll be sure to pass on the message.

MARGARET: Oh, I don't believe you two!

CHARLOTTE: We'll see you off at the train then.

BILL: If you wish. Lovely day. *(He exits.)*

> *MARGARET stares at CHARLOTTE for a moment, takes her drum and the picnic stuff away. CHARLOTTE sits on the floor, lost in thought. EMILY enters.*

EMILY: Gee! Miss Whitton! Are you okay? *(She goes to help her up.)* Did you fall down?

CHARLOTTE: That was fast.

EMILY: I ran.

CHARLOTTE: How energetic of you.

EMILY: I found it, though.

CHARLOTTE: What did you find?

EMILY: The tune. I found it.

CHARLOTTE: Really? Hum a few bars.

MARGARET: Charlotte.

EMILY: Okay. Let's see... *(Hums a few bars. MARGARET hums with her.)* It's called "The Honeysuckle and the Bee."

MARGARET: That's the name of it!

EMILY: There was a band playing it in the park.

CHARLOTTE: Oh.

EMILY: I'm not sure how the words go, but I could probably find out if you really want—

MARGARET: *(Singing.)* "You are my honeysuckle, I am the bee, I'd like to sip the honey sweet from those red lips, you see..."

CHARLOTTE: No, no it's not necessary. I remember how it goes now.

MARGARET: *"I love you dearly dearly and I want you to love me. You are my honey, honeysuckle, I am the bee..."*

CHARLOTTE: You must be thirsty after all that running. Here let's have another. *(She pours more drinks—EMILY drinks hers right down.)* Now, where were we?

EMILY: You were telling me about the friends you had to leave behind. In order to follow your heart's desire. And saying goodbye to Bill for the last time.

CHARLOTTE: Bill?

MARGARET: Selective memory.

EMILY: Bidding farewell to your sweetheart, not knowing if the two of you would ever cross paths again. *(Pouring herself another glass—she drinks.)* I know what that's like.

CHARLOTTE: Perhaps you should try sipping.

EMILY: When I left home to go to school I had to say goodbye to someone. For some reason, I was so scared. It was as if the distance was going to be a kind of death. And it was. *(She drinks.)*

Sound of a train whistle.

EMILY: Oh, that sound. *(She's a little tipsy now as she goes to look out the window.)* I love the sound of the train. Wooo wooo! Oh gosh, I wish I could write sound. No matter what words one uses to describe certain sounds, they can never capture the real thing. The longing, the melancholy ache as it chugs away into the distance. Wooo wooo! *(She spills some drink onto the curtains.)* Oh dear.

> EMILY dabs at the curtains. The train whistle blows again. An old dance tune starts playing. ("Honeysuckle and the Bee.")
>
> MARGARET starts dancing.

CHARLOTTE: What are you doing?

EMILY: I spilt.

MARGARET: I'm dancing.

CHARLOTTE: Why?

EMILY: I'm just clumsy, I guess.

MARGARET: It's what I always used to do whenever I saw you off at the train. I knew I was going to be sad, so I just danced myself happy. Now whenever I hear the whistle, I can't help it.

> Train whistle blows again.
>
> MARGARET dances to a corner of the stage and we are in a train station. 1918. BILL enters the platform at the train station with their bags.

BILL: (Throwing his bag down.) I could strangle that woman!

CHARLOTTE: He didn't say that!

MARGARET: You're not here yet.

BILL: (Throwing his bag down again.) I could strangle that woman!

MARGARET: Oh now, Bill, you must be patient with her—she always insists on carrying her own bags.

BILL: The woman is no bigger than a large child. You'd think that this once she could allow me to carry something—or hire a porter if she's too proud!

MARGARET: Charlotte is very frugal, Bill. A porter would be out of the question.

BILL: I'll pay for the damned porter!

MARGARET: *(Sighs.)* How on earth will she ever manage without you, Bill?

BILL: Yes, I'm terribly worried that Toronto will...overwhelm her.

MARGARET: I'm going to miss her too. We do plan to keep in touch, though. And you, Bill? You will write to her? She doesn't show it much, but I know that Charlotte is just sick about you having to go overseas.

BILL: Is she? I would have thought she would see it as my duty to Canada.

MARGARET: We must all do our duty.

> *CHARLOTTE enters with a lot of bags, feigning exhaustion. She drops them—all the while glaring at BILL.*

CHARLOTTE: Well, you could have offered the lady a hand.

BILL: Ahhhh!

MARGARET: She's goading you, Bill.

BILL: *(To CHARLOTTE.)* I'm getting a porter. And not one word of protest from you. *(He exits.)*

CHARLOTTE: He's very nerved.

MARGARET: He's worried that Toronto will overwhelm you.

CHARLOTTE: Is he now?

MARGARET: He called you a large child.

CHARLOTTE: Atta boy!

MARGARET: I don't want to think of it, but we may never see Bill again, Charlotte.

CHARLOTTE: Don't think of it. He's too stubborn to lose the war. Look at the poor fellow. Who could shoot him?

MARGARET: Charlotte, it's too real.

CHARLOTTE: Oh gracious, Margaret. I'm sorry. You really are worried.

> *Suddenly MARGARET reaches out and holds CHARLOTTE by the arm. They look at each other.*

Oh. I'm going to miss that face.

MARGARET: You will be too busy in Toronto to think of my face.

CHARLOTTE: I have an inclination that your face will be etched on the sidewalks, Margaret.

MARGARET: Oh well, don't be stepping on me then.

CHARLOTTE: And in the reflections on the windows of the buildings.

MARGARET: Oh my.

CHARLOTTE: In the water that flows from the fountains and on the sheets of paper on which I will be writing to you.

MARGARET: If my face is on the paper, be mindful of my nose when you write.

CHARLOTTE: Such a beautiful nose.

> *CHARLOTTE touches MARGARET's nose. MARGARET takes her hand.*

MARGARET: I look forward to your letters, Charlotte. You always say things just right. I'm afraid that I won't be able to express myself to you in a letter.

CHARLOTTE: You just have to be honest. Write to me as if you were speaking to me.

MARGARET: Charlotte, I don't know how to say this now, but I feel—

BILL enters.

BILL: The porter is on his way.

MARGARET: I'll leave you two alone to say your goodbyes.

CHARLOTTE: Margaret! Wait. *(Pulling MARGARET aside.)* You will come back for a proper goodbye.

MARGARET: If there is such a thing as a proper goodbye?

CHARLOTTE: What was it you wanted to say?

BILL: What are you two plotting?

MARGARET: I feel…as though I should get my ticket arranged. Excuse me. *(She exits.)*

CHARLOTTE: I'll help you…

BILL: Ah ah ah. I don't trust you two alone. You're liable to bring down the station manager and tell him how to run the place.

He grabs CHARLOTTE by the hand and swings her into his arms. A rather awkward embrace.

Oh, Charlotte. Charlotte. I will write to you every day, I promise. And please, try not worry too much about me. I want you to promise not to worry yourself into a frenzy.

CHARLOTTE: I promise, Bill.

BILL: I'm mad about you, Lottie, I really am. I can't believe I feel like this.

CHARLOTTE: It really is remarkable to feel so deeply for someone.

Molly's Veil

BILL: Do you mean that, Charlotte?

CHARLOTTE: What. What?

BILL: Knowing that you feel deeply for me will get me through this damned war.

CHARLOTTE: If knowing that will help you, Bill, then…know it.

BILL: I will. I do. Oh, Charlotte. I know it.

Pause— they look at each other.

BILL: I can't believe what's happening to me… It's all so mysterious. I so look forward to your letters.

CHARLOTTE: I will be writing a lot of them.

The train whistle blows.

BILL: That's mine, I think. I better…I don't know what's become of that porter.

CHARLOTTE: Hang the porter.

BILL: Hang the porter. Ha ha. Yes…I don't think he would appreciate that much.

CHARLOTTE: Bill. Take care, Bill. I will write to you. And I promise not to worry.

BILL takes her hand and kisses it.

MARGARET: *(Enters hurriedly.)* Bill. I heard your whistle. Oh, take care love. Do give them what for over there. *(She embraces him.)*

BILL: Goodbye, Margaret. *(BILL exits.)*

MARGARET: I hate goodbyes.

CHARLOTTE: Well then, we won't say goodbye, we'll say hello. It will be our code. Our way of telling each other that being apart is actually the beginning of being even closer together.

MARGARET: Hello then.

CHARLOTTE: Hello. What was it that you wanted to say to me before?

MARGARET: Just hello.

> *CHARLOTTE picks up her bags and exits while MARGARET waves her away. MARGARET is happily waving until CHARLOTTE gets out of sight and then she begins to cry. She sobs and sobs and the train whistle continues to blow. MARGARET tries to dance. She starts tentatively at first and slowly finds a way to "dance herself happy." CHARLOTTE is struck by the strange bravery of the moment. EMILY is crying and blowing her nose.*

CHARLOTTE: What on earth is the matter with you?

EMILY: Goodbyes. I just can't take goodbyes. I can't believe I spilled on your mayoral drapes. How embarrassing.

She blows her nose again.

CHARLOTTE: Well, that should improve their mayoral aroma.

EMILY: I'm sorry. This isn't very professional of me.

CHARLOTTE: If those drapes could speak, I feel certain they would forgive you.

EMILY: Do you think so? *(To the drapes.)* I'm sorry I spilt on you.

MARGARET: She's talking to the drapes.

CHARLOTTE: It appears so.

EMILY: *(Still to the drapes.)* You're very pretty, I'm sure that once you have a proper cleaning you'll be good as new again. That's a lovely pattern... *(She keeps on talking.)*

MARGARET: You really do bring out the best in people, Charlotte.

CHARLOTTE: There was a time when you believed that to be true.

MARGARET: There was a time when it was true.

CHARLOTTE: I didn't know you liked dancing so much.

MARGARET: I learned to love it. I had to.

Pause.

CHARLOTTE: Let's see if we can get her to start speaking to something else. The typewriter!

MARGARET: Charlotte—

CHARLOTTE: It will be funny. Oh Miss Wicks?

EMILY: I think I can get it out, I just need some washing powder.

CHARLOTTE: I want to show you something.

EMILY: Miss Whitton, didn't it make you sad? Leaving school and your friends like that?

Pause.

MARGARET: Well?

CHARLOTTE: We wrote letters to one another.

MARGARET: You didn't answer the question. *(She goes to the typewriter.)* Do you want to write a letter? I'll put some paper in the typewriter.

EMILY: Oh no, I don't want to write any letters.

MARGARET: You never saw me dancing because you were always going away.

CHARLOTTE: Or, we don't even need to use paper. You could just…speak your thoughts.

Sharon Bajer

EMILY: My...thoughts?

CHARLOTTE: Maybe there is a friend you wish to speak to.

EMILY: A friend? No.

CHARLOTTE: No one, no one from your childhood?

MARGARET: You don't know what to say.

EMILY: There is one person, but no. I wouldn't know what to say. We haven't spoken since I left to go to school. It wouldn't be right.

CHARLOTTE: What would you say to this person, if they were standing in front of you right now?

EMILY: But they're not. It's just a typewriter.

CHARLOTTE: What kind of a journalist are you? You've got to use some imagination!

EMILY: I do need some paper I think.

CHARLOTTE: Of course! Now, this should go here and...blast! Cursed glorified paperweight! *(She starts putting the paper in and gets frustrated.)*

MARGARET: Now who's talking to the typewriter?

EMILY: Okay. Here it goes.

She starts typing.

EMILY's VOICE: Dear Roger—

MARGARET's VOICE: Dear Charlotte—

BILL's VOICE: Dear Lottie—

EMILY's VOICE: I know the last time we saw each other was long ago—

MARGARET's
VOICE: Just two nights gone and I'm so lonesome I could cry whenever I stop to think for a minute—

BILL's VOICE: I know you must be ready for some humour, so let me tell you about a little furry visitor I had on my first night here—

MARGARET: *(From a farm in Northern Ontario, 1918.)* What perfectly lovely letters you write to me, Lottie. When I was a youngster I used to ask Dad why, when you loved a person, you wanted to hug them with all your strength. I have never had a satisfying answer. I think it's a primeval, cannibal sort of feeling where you like and admire something very much and you want to get it inside you. Lottie, I must confess that I am deeply, head over heels in love with you and it expresses itself in an overpowering desire to devour you, at your throat of course! When you are famous I will tell my friends how I used to enjoy kissing the authoress on the neck and how I have even slept in her arms. Even... I would have replied earlier, but both of my parents are in the "grips of influenza" and require a lot of attention from their offspring...

BILL: *(In the trenches.)* Oh Charlotte. I can't tell you what a joy it was to receive your letter. I'm glad that you are settling in all right and that I haven't left you too lonely. Thank you for the article. It was very nice to get some news from home. Your description of the landscape from Ottawa to Toronto was very vivid. I felt as though I had been travelling with you. And that was a funny story about the rabbit. I really had a good laugh over that. Laughter is a scarcity around here. Charlotte, forgive me if I seemed a little overzealous before my departure. I was overcome by it all I think, but I do hope you don't think me a lecher or anything. Ha ha. I have nothing but the most honorable intentions...I know you don't like me to talk about that. Hmm. I think of you often. Only the purest of thoughts of course. You are my lifeline right now, Charlotte.

Pause.

BILL: Your friend, Bill.

EMILY's VOICE: Sincerely, Emily.

MARGARET: Eves of our loving, Margaret.

EMILY: There. I did it.

CHARLOTTE: Hm…what's that?

EMILY: My letter. I finished it. I don't think I could ever send it though. Oh dear.

CHARLOTTE: What's the matter now?

EMILY: It's just, well, imagination does stir things up. I'm all flushed.

CHARLOTTE: Why don't you read it out?

EMILY: No! I couldn't do that! It's private.

CHARLOTTE: Private is it? Even better.

MARGARET: Why don't you read her some letters from your book?

CHARLOTTE: It's private.

MARGARET: Tit for tat!

EMILY: Yes, it is. Ms. Whitton, can I ask you something? Not for the article, but just between um…"sisters." Did you *ever* consider marriage?

CHARLOTTE: To whom.

EMILY: Bill King, of course, your sweetheart.

MARGARET: Well?

CHARLOTTE: Women who try to raise children and carry on in the workplace are mad, and their children become sorely neglected.

MARGARET: They're not the only ones.

EMILY: Yes, you've always said that.

CHARLOTTE: You've done well not trying to do both.

EMILY: Everyone I know is having children.

MARGARET: Why don't you tell her the real reason you didn't marry your sweetheart?

CHARLOTTE: Margaret!

EMILY: What happened to her?

CHARLOTTE: Who?

EMILY: Your friend Margaret. I was going to ask you. Did you ever see her again after your time at Queen's?

MARGARET: Well?

CHARLOTTE: Yes.

MARGARET: And?

CHARLOTTE: And…

MARGARET: Go on.

CHARLOTTE: She had been living with her ailing parents—

MARGARET: On the farm—

CHARLOTTE: On a farm of all places. Completely isolated and cut off from any of her peers.

MARGARET: I had the chickens.

CHARLOTTE: With only chickens for company.

MARGARET: And then?

CHARLOTTE: I could tell from her letters that something was wrong.

MARGARET: Then—

CHARLOTTE: Then, one day she—

MARGARET: Lopped all the chickens' heads off while headed for church.

CHARLOTTE: —had a crisis of faith.

MARGARET: Don't clean it up like that. I sat in my Sunday best, covered in blood, axe in my hand and listened to the sound of their headless bodies running around. I just sat there and didn't move until the chickens had run themselves out. My parents thought I was crazy.

CHARLOTTE: She ended up having to go to the—

MARGARET: Loony bin.

CHARLOTTE: —hospital. She was exhausted. I took the train up to see her right away.

MARGARET: I was so happy to see you.

CHARLOTTE: She looked so small and frail lying in that room.

MARGARET: You brought me a book of Yeats.

CHARLOTTE: Being back in Kingston reminded me how much I had missed the river valley. So when the Child Welfare Commission was relocated to Ottawa, I decided to go with it.

MARGARET: The river valley? You missed the river valley?

CHARLOTTE: Margaret got a job with the Boy Scouts and we found a flat together that was quite cheap. Two incomes to mind a household seemed far more practical.

MARGARET: You sure tell a good story.

EMILY: I had a roommate once, but she ended up getting married.

MARGARET: I can't believe you can stand to hear yourself talk.

EMILY: Miss Whitton, did Bill ever marry?

CHARLOTTE: Bill? No.

MARGARET: Because you never told the truth.

EMILY: You don't have any regrets?

CHARLOTTE: I have only one regret and it follows me everywhere!

MARGARET: You can let me go at any time.

EMILY: Does it fade with time?

CHARLOTTE: It feeds on time.

MARGARET: It's because you will it that way. I can leave at any time. But it's up to you.

CHARLOTTE: Why don't you then? Why don't you stop following me and just go away? You brought me my statue. I'll just talk to Elizabeth now. It's the same thing after all, isn't it? You're not real! I can do with you what I like!

MARGARET: I'm not real?

EMILY: That's good! *(Going up to the typewriter and yelling at it.)* Why don't you just go! Stop making me think about you all the time! I wrote you the damn letter, what more do you want? Stop following me around and just go away! You're not even real! Wow, that feels good!

CHARLOTTE: Who are you talking to?

EMILY: Roger Elton. The only man I've ever kissed. We were supposed to be married and I left him to go to school. But I don't know if I did the right thing.

MARGARET: "You've always said to choose between a husband or a job and to not try to have both." Those are your very words. Words this woman has lived by her entire life! Show her the book!

EMILY: Sometimes I get so lonely I just want to scream.

MARGARET: Or are those lies too?

CHARLOTTE: Right now I could just scream to be alone!

EMILY: Don't you want me to stay?

MARGARET: Do you want me to go?

CHARLOTTE: Yes! In the name of God, yes!

EMILY: Okay.

MARGARET: Okay. I'll go. If you really are the woman you say you are, you can erase me straight out of your life. Go right ahead!

Silence.

Maybe you are right about your achievements, Mayor Whitton. Maybe they are the only things that remain with you in the end. (*She exits.*)

EMILY: Miss Whitton, can I tell you something, honestly? I was really afraid to meet you today. I've admired you so much. Your words are what gave me the strength to keep on—even on those really lonely days. Like you, I wanted to do something important with my life. (*Pause.*) Miss. Whitton? Are you all right?

CHARLOTTE: What are you blithering on about?

EMILY: I was saying, I don't know what made me so nervous meeting you at first. It's like I was afraid you would think I was silly, or girlish somehow.

CHARLOTTE: I do think that.

EMILY: Oh.

CHARLOTTE: You'd have been better off as a baby machine on a farm. You'll never make it as a journalist.

EMILY: I'm sorry?

CHARLOTTE: Go ahead and send that letter, or better yet, take the night train back to whatever small town you most likely come from, I'm sure it's not too late. Those country bumpkins can hold out for quite a while.

EMILY: I don't understand?!

CHARLOTTE: Go ask Rodney your inane questions. I'm sure he'd find you very sophisticated. Perhaps *Time* magazine could use him as their cover boy.

EMILY: I thought you wanted me to stay?

CHARLOTTE: I've changed my mind!

EMILY: Are you…kicking me out?

CHARLOTTE: If you prefer.

EMILY: But we've only just begun. You can't do this!

CHARLOTTE: I can do what I like. I'm the mayor.

EMILY: Miss Whitton, I try really hard to get people to take me seriously. I thought you of all people would understand…

CHARLOTTE: I have no one now.

EMILY: I know what you mean!

CHARLOTTE: No, you don't know what I mean! What are you? A parrot? You say that because you believe it will somehow bond us into sharing intimate secrets!

EMILY: That's not true!

CHARLOTTE: Isn't that what they teach you at journalism school!

	To say whatever it takes to get the subject to trust you?
EMILY:	But I—
CHARLOTTE:	To uncover personal matters?
EMILY:	I thought—
CHARLOTTE:	To find an angle?
EMILY:	But I really *do* know what you mean.
CHARLOTTE:	Look what you've done, you've disrupted my time—distracting me! You're poking at me, prodding, shaking all the shingles loose! Get out! Get out before the whole roof collapses!
EMILY:	I'm sorry! I'm so sorry that I upset you! I just thought…I shouldn't have drunk. I'm so stupid! I'm sorry! *(She exits.)*
CHARLOTTE:	Margaret Jean Grier you show yourself immediately! Margaret! You can't just do that. You can't just have it your way! Tell me, what have I done? So I don't want to read the silly girl my book. It's none of anyone's business! Margaret! Margaret! Okay, Margaret, okay. Which bits? Which bits would satisfy you? *(She opens the book.)* No answer? Then I'll start at the beginning. Dearest. This will be the first of the new and empty years in which I shall go on alone. Is this what you want, Margaret? It is late New Year's Eve and I am on the train to Edmonton. I know so well that my way will go on for a long time on this side of the veil. Do stay close and walk with me step by step on the other. You and God know the light and peace I denied you by not getting in that room and clasping your poor stealing body… Oh! Mardie! Mardie! How can I go on? Ours wasn't love…It was a knitting together of mind and spirit…It was something given to few by God. There wasn't

anything silly or weak in sharing; it was just that our minds and spirits marched so together that they were the same in two different bodies. And here in the body part, mine stays, numb and bewildered, while yours soars away. Margaret? Oh, please come back! I'll call the girl back! I'll tell her everything! Just please come home! I'll promise anything, just show yourself to me!

ELIZABETH's
VOICE: Lottie?

CHARLOTTE: Who said that?

ELIZABETH: This isn't a very becoming way for a woman of office to behave.

> *CHARLOTTE screams.*
>
> *Blackout.*

Act II

A cottage at McGregor Lake, Ontario. CHARLOTTE's desk sits in the corner of the room with a typewriter. There is a wood stove. CHARLOTTE is asleep in a rocking chair clutching the book with a afghan tucked around her. She awakes with a start and hears a chopping sound outside and the sound of a chicken running around with its head cut off. Just then the door to the cottage bursts open and EMILY with a dead chicken and an axe. CHARLOTTE screams.

EMILY: Oh, you're up! I tried to wake you when I got up this morning, but you were just dead to the world.

CHARLOTTE: We came up last night?

EMILY: Well, I suppose technically it was very early this morning when we arrived.

CHARLOTTE: Oh, yes, of course. I'm a bit cobwebby.

EMILY: It's no wonder you're disoriented—when we got here you went straight to that chair and fell instantly asleep. I tried to wake you so that you could sleep in a proper bed, but you were already starting to dream I think—or having a nightmare it sounded like. *(She puts some firewood into the stove.)*

CHARLOTTE: Did I...say anything?

EMILY: Just calling for your friend Margaret.

CHARLOTTE: I was calling for Margaret?

EMILY: Yes.

CHARLOTTE: Did you...see her anywhere?

EMILY: Well, this cottage is filled with her. I slept in her room I think. The green one. *(Picking up a photograph on the mantel.)* Is this is her? She's very pretty. And is this your little dog?

CHARLOTTE: Rusty.

EMILY: Aww. She's so cute. Do you still have her?

CHARLOTTE: Him. Yes. He's buried in the yard under the white lilac.

EMILY: I'm so glad you suggested we come out here! It's lovely.

CHARLOTTE: Yes.

EMILY: I was beginning to think that you hated me.

CHARLOTTE: Miss Wicks, I think I said some dreadful things to you yesterday.

EMILY: I kind of deserved it. It was a big day for me and I just messed it all up. I'm grateful that you decided to let me start over. Spending a few days here with you will give such a rustic touch to the profile. I don't think anyone would have pegged you for a country bumpkin.

CHARLOTTE: Please, let's not get off on the *other* wrong foot.

EMILY: Sorry. Oops, I got a little blood on the photo. I better wash up before I get blood on everything! Um...can I get you anything—tea?

CHARLOTTE: Will it take you out of here for a moment?

EMILY: Well, I'd have to find something to put the water in. Oh, and the chicken.

CHARLOTTE: Then tea would be extraordinary.

EMILY exits. CHARLOTTE takes in the cottage, touching some of the objects—she hasn't been here in some time. She picks up the photo and tries to rub off the blood that EMILY left there.

Margaret? Margaret! Are you here? I'm sorry about yesterday. I'm sorry I neglected you—I tried so hard to explain things to you in my last letter to avoid all this, darling. It was foolish of me to try and keep you away. Please. Margaret. I just can't bear not hearing your voice! *(She opens the book and reads.)*

CHARLOTTE: Dearest—

VOICE 2: Dear Putty—

MARGARET's
VOICE: Mardie—

VOICE 1: Margaret—

VOICE 2: Redcat—

CHARLOTTE: Wee pussy—

ALL: Darling…

CHARLOTTE: I am on board and sailing on a Bay of Fundy that is so supernaturally calm as to be almost ominous.

MARGARET's
VOICE: I have a very nice cabin, a lovely stewardess and a nice steward. Everything is orderly and not filthy like the Halifax docks.

VOICE 1: The St. John people were really very nice to me. I got roses, sweet peas and spring flowers from them, including some white iris which I had never seen before…

VOICE 2: I shall be in Florence but a day, then I must return to Geneva to broadcast to Canada. I hope you will hear me…

CHARLOTTE: I would like to say a word to you, but I suppose that will not be allowed...

ALL: Oh! Dear! But I wish you were here!

CHARLOTTE & MARGARET: I do miss you so!

VOICE 2: And when the best paper said that Ottawa was all flooded along the Rideau to Russell Road—

VOICE 1: —I did so hope my cat, who is so fond of messing around in boats would not go out in a tub just for fun...

CHARLOTTE: I wanted to be with you yesterday when women officially became persons.

MARGARET's VOICE: It's funny, I don't feel any different now that I'm officially a person.

VOICE 2: I'll certainly be expecting a poem about it when I come home.

CHARLOTTE: I miss you every moment I am away...

MARGARET's VOICE: And when I write to you...

VOICE 1: It's almost as if you're with me, taking in the beauty of it all...

CHARLOTTE: I wish I could share it with you today...

ALL: Love on love—

VOICE 2: Your "hot cross bunny"—

CHARLOTTE: Charles—

MARGARET's VOICE: Charlie—

VOICE 1: Rags—

VOICE 2: Dee Wee—

ALL: Molly, Lottie, Charl, Petit Chou…

CHARLOTTE: …and it was always so lovely to return home again—where you would be waiting. My red cat. My rock of ages.

She gets her pen and begins a new page.

CHARLOTTE: Dear Margaret: Last night we drove up here together in my dreams—you in the blueberry suit I gave you. Margaret darling, will you not come today too? I'll close my eyes and you can surprise me like I did to you the first time you saw this place.

(*She closes her eyes.*) And you said…you said, "Charl, can I open my eyes now?" And I said "No, not quite yet" and you said… "Now, Charl" and I said "Not just yet, don't be so impatient" and you bumped into a tree and I said… "For pity sake, you're going to trip over a bramble!" And you said…

1930. MARGARET enters with her eyes closed.

MARGARET: What on earth is a bramble?

CHARLOTTE: You're here!

MARGARET: Can I open them now?

CHARLOTTE: Margaret?

MARGARET: Can I open them now?

CHARLOTTE: Can you hear me? Margaret?

MARGARET: Can I open them now?

CHARLOTTE: Yes Mardie, you can open your eyes now.

MARGARET: *(Opening her eyes and looking at the place for the first time.)* Oh, Lottie! It's so beautiful! But do you really think we can afford it?

CHARLOTTE: You like it?

MARGARET: It's really lovely, Charl, but I just don't know how we're going to manage it.

CHARLOTTE: Well, the most important thing for you is rest and a place for you to regain your health. Come, I want to show you your garden. We can have some earth brought in to raise these beds around the house and there is your potting shed. It will need a little fixing up, but there is a lovely Jim who lives just down the lane who has offered to help and he'll also set you up with some running water back in the back. There's plenty of room for a vegetable garden and we have all the land up to that big elm there. We can have a fence put up to define it more, but I knew you'd want a say in that.

MARGARET: I don't know what to say, this is like a little piece of heaven!

CHARLOTTE: Yes, it's a pleasant spot isn't it?

MARGARET: No, I mean—the place—yes it is, but, Charlotte, this is our home—our home—together!

BOTH: Ahhhh!

They grab each other and spin around laughing.

CHARLOTTE: We can be as silly as we want here!

MARGARET: And walk around in our frilly drawers!

CHARLOTTE: Look Margaret! Our stove!

MARGARET: Hello, stove! And our watering can!

CHARLOTTE: Hello, watering can!

MARGARET: And our tea cups! *(She holds them in front of her breasts.)*

CHARLOTTE: Hello, cups!

They giggle hysterically.

Now, of course, you know that I can't stop my travelling, so I thought that you might need some company.

MARGARET: Oh, you don't have to worry, I'm sure I'll meet plenty of people. What are you doing?

CHARLOTTE: *(Has gotten down on all fours and is sniffing around.)* What am I?

MARGARET: A very silly woman?

CHARLOTTE: *(Getting a slipper and shaking it around in her mouth.)* I'm being something. What am I?

MARGARET: You're a seal with a big salmon head in its mouth!

CHARLOTTE: No. *(She sits up and begs with her paws.)*

MARGARET: A lioness gesturing to her cubs to get down because a hunter is approaching.

CHARLOTTE: How on earth do you get that from that? I'm a puppy, for heaven's sake!

MARGARET: Wonderful! What other tricks can you do?

CHARLOTTE: Open the slipper. Look inside.

MARGARET: *(Taking a photograph out of the slipper.)* Oh, look at them. Aren't they cute?

CHARLOTTE: Keely's aunt has a litter of newborn pups and I thought you'd like to pick one out and we'll bring him out here when they're old enough to leave the mom.

MARGARET: Oh really! Well, it would have to be that one.

CHARLOTTE: I was hoping you'd pick that one. She's a redhead. Like you! Rusty. Rusty. We can call her Rusty!

CHARLOTTE: Or him, if it's a he.

MARGARET: Either way, Rusty fits. I love him already.

CHARLOTTE: Now when I go away, I won't have to worry about you having one of your spells, now will I?

MARGARET: Oh no, Charlotte, I will be very happy with all this.

CHARLOTTE: You really gave me a scare last time, Margaret.

MARGARET: I know, luv, but you needn't worry now. It's going to be good for us here, I have a feeling.

CHARLOTTE: Come on, I want to show you your green room. It's very exotic. After you, Madame. *(MARGARET exits to the bedroom, but EMILY breaks the memory by coming out of the room with a bucket.)*

EMILY: Found a bucket!

CHARLOTTE: No! Don't go yet!

EMILY: I'll be right back. I'm going to get some water for the tea. I'm assuming the pump still works?

CHARLOTTE: Yes.

EMILY: It's great to have the fresh air. I grew up in the country. It brings back so many cozy memories.

CHARLOTTE: Mmm.

EMILY: I've spent so much time in the city, I was beginning to think I had a deficiency of some kind.

CHARLOTTE: Did you just use deficiency in a sentence?

EMILY: Pardon me?

CHARLOTTE: The country dairy air is good for your vocabulary Miss Wicks.

EMILY: *(Laughing.)*

CHARLOTTE: What's so funny?

EMILY: You just used "country derriere" in a sentence.

CHARLOTTE: I suppose I did.

EMILY: Well, I'm going to take my country derriere out in to the country dairy air to get some water for our tea.

CHARLOTTE: You do that.

EMILY exits.

CHARLOTTE: Margaret? Did you hear that? The girl has a glimmer of wit! Margaret? Blast! Show yourself to me! For real, not in a smoke screen of pieces. Margaret! Why won't you talk to me?

April, 1934. MARGARET enters with a ledger.

MARGARET: Charlotte? Is that you?

CHARLOTTE: Margaret? Oh! How I missed you, you little crosspatch!

MARGARET: You look like you need a good scratch.

CHARLOTTE: No. Margaret. Talk to me for real.

MARGARET: You look like you need a good scratch.

CHARLOTTE: Blast, Margaret! All right then. What are you doing up, Mardie?

MARGARET: I must have been sleepwalking.

CHARLOTTE: I hope you didn't wait up for me half the night.

MARGARET: I guess I just lost track of time.

CHARLOTTE: Did you get my telegram?

MARGARET: Yes.

CHARLOTTE: So you knew not to expect me until today.

MARGARET: I must have got it mixed up. I wanted to be looking nice at least when you came in.

CHARLOTTE: No, no, you look beautiful all fuzzy like that. It was really not at all a pleasant trip without you.

MARGARET: You don't have to say that.

CHARLOTTE: Where's Rusty?

MARGARET: He chews the rug so badly when you're away, I've had to put him in his house for the night.

CHARLOTTE: Poor thing. I'll have to go out to him. What do you have there?

MARGARET: *(Sitting on the ledger she has been holding.)* Nothing.

CHARLOTTE: Margaret, I just want to look at it.

MARGARET: At what, darling?

CHARLOTTE: At the ledger currently holding up your fanny.

She grabs it from under her.

MARGARET: Oh no, give me that back!

CHARLOTTE: I'm not doing anything. I just wanted to see what you were up to while I was away.

MARGARET: It isn't a blasted diary—for heaven's sake!

CHARLOTTE: Oh no, I disagree. There must be some reason you don't want me to look at it, or you wouldn't be so anxious to have it back.

MARGARET: I'm not anxious. Now can I please have it back my darling?

CHARLOTTE: In a moment, my sweet. I just want to peruse the expenditures of the past few weeks. What did you do…throw a party….buy a yacht? I'm so curious.

(She opens the ledger and turns the pages. She is shocked by what she sees.) Margaret, what is this?

MARGARET: Well, It's...nothing.

CHARLOTTE: I can see that Margaret Jean, but where are the accounts figures?

MARGARET: What does it say there?

CHARLOTTE: This is the alphabet, Margaret. On every page.

MARGARET: I just started and I couldn't stop and before I knew it, I had filled the book. And it's in ink.

CHARLOTTE: I can see that. Did you perchance record our expenses elsewhere then?

MARGARET: No, Charlotte, I did not.

CHARLOTTE: May I ask why?

MARGARET: I needed a break from thinking about every damned penny. It got so I couldn't eat a cracker without seeing a figure on it.

CHARLOTTE: You knew when you decided not to work that we would have to be careful with money.

MARGARET: Decided! I had no choice!

CHARLOTTE: Ah, so this is it. You are *not* working and I *am* and you have to *mind the house* while I'm off *gallivanting*—we've been through all this before. It's my *work* that takes me. I have to *work* so that we can afford to keep this place.

MARGARET: But you love to work!

CHARLOTTE: It's a sin to love one's work?

MARGARET: No, yes! You're always leaving me.

CHARLOTTE: And I always come back. That's what's so

wonderful. You are my home, my hearth. It's all meaningless without you.

MARGARET: You *say* that. But then I'm always left alone with letters describing the most interesting places and people.

CHARLOTTE: I thought you loved my letters!

MARGARET: I do!

CHARLOTTE: So what do I do, Margaret? Stay home with you so that you can complain about my wearing shoes in the house or not minding your forget-me-nots between the garden stones. I can't stay at home for long periods of time. It puts you off your routine. It would drive both you and me crazy.

MARGARET: Charlotte!

CHARLOTTE: No, I'm sorry, love—I didn't mean to use that word.

MARGARET: You think that I *am* crazy!

CHARLOTTE: No. No. Not in the negative sense of the word.

MARGARET: There's a positive sense?

CHARLOTTE: You're just more vulnerable to life's daily disappointments than most people. Let's just forget about it. I'll take care of the records from now on. We must have the next trip together. *(She pulls out a small box.)* I've brought you a present. From Geneva.

MARGARET: *(Opening it.)* What on earth?

CHARLOTTE: It's a newfangled cigarette lighter.

MARGARET: Do you think I should take up smoking?

CHARLOTTE: Good heavens, no! I just...thought you might find it amusing.

MARGARET: *(Tries the lighter a few times and stares at the flame for a bit—doesn't find it amusing.)* Hm.

CHARLOTTE: Well?

MARGARET: *(Unimpressed.)* It's very nice.

CHARLOTTE: You don't like it.

MARGARET: These presents are late. You missed my birthday.

CHARLOTTE: Margaret! For heaven's sake! I don't know what else I could have done! The whole thing was entirely out of my hands, you know that!

MARGARET: Yes, of course, Lott. I'm just glad you're home safe and sound.

CHARLOTTE: You don't sound glad.

MARGARET: Just say that you're sorry. That's all I want.

CHARLOTTE: That's all you want?

MARGARET: Yes.

CHARLOTTE: All right! I'm sorry I missed your birthday!

MARGARET: You don't sound sorry.

CHARLOTTE: Well, I don't know what more I can say. I'm sorry. I'm sorry. They will write it on my tombstone, "Margaret, I'm sorry."

MARGARET: You shouldn't say those things.

CHARLOTTE: Tell me, what *can* I say then?

MARGARET: If you don't know, I'm not going to tell you.

CHARLOTTE: I'm sorry I missed your birthday again, Margaret.

MARGARET: That's not all you're going to miss.

CHARLOTTE: What?

MARGARET: Nothing, it's not important.

CHARLOTTE: Margaret!

MARGARET: I'm sorry. I'll get over it. Just give me a day to get used to you again. *(Pause.)* You look so well. I missed your face. Here, let's light something—a candle! *(They light a candle.)* Now tell me about your trip.

CHARLOTTE: Oh, the sessions in Geneva were intolerable—Persia, China and Turkey are messy additions to the League committee—

MARGARET: Imagine you at the League of Nations!

CHARLOTTE: And Chile is a weak sister. But India is fantastic! They sent a Mrs. Subbarayan, a splendid Hindi woman, graduate of Oxford. She speaks well, thinks clearly, and some of the other countries are undoubtedly scared of her. She adds heartily to British strength and wears the most gorgeous saris and jewels.

MARGARET: She seems to have made quite an impression on you.

CHARLOTTE: Oh, Mardie, you know how much I love glitter. India is an exotic country. We will visit together when you are well again.

MARGARET: Mm, I would like that.

CHARLOTTE: Do you need anything? Tea?

MARGARET: Yes, please. *(CHARLOTTE starts toward the kitchen.)* Charlotte!

CHARLOTTE: What?

MARGARET: Tell me about the Prince!

CHARLOTTE: Ah…the prince! How could I forget? You see, love, not even the Prince puts you out of my head.

MARGARET: I'm flattered. But tell me. How was it? What happened—tell me everything!

CHARLOTTE: Well, I'm still in a dither about it. It seemed so unreal. Over half an hour in private audience with the Prince of Wales—all by myself. I am not yet even conscious! I feel that I made a blithering arse of myself, but he was very nice—and such a flock of questions he asked me! I nearly died! And at one point I called him "Your Majesty" when I meant to say "His Majesty, your father" —so I only hope I didn't say "Your Majesty, his father." Ahhh!

MARGARET: But more importantly, what did you wear?!

CHARLOTTE: Well, a suit was in order so I bought a nice tailored gray flannel—I could have done without otherwise. I had my suede shoes cleaned and gloves to match.

MARGARET: Lovely!

CHARLOTTE: And, the blouse you brought me from the north.

MARGARET: Oh, it's almost as if I was there too.

CHARLOTTE: I knew you would be glad.

MARGARET: Ever so!

CHARLOTTE: And I knew I'd feel safer with something old and beloved on, and it made me feel that you were backing me.

MARGARET: Oh yes, indeed! *(Pause.)* Charlotte—you met the Prince!

CHARLOTTE: Yes, I have done.

BOTH: Ahhhh!

EMILY: *(EMILY enters with the bucket of water.)* Tea will be ready in a minute.

CHARLOTTE: *(To MARGARET.)* You see how I have her trained.

MARGARET: *(Doesn't look at her or respond, she just walks off.)*

CHARLOTTE: Why can't you hear me?

EMILY: Sorry?

CHARLOTTE: Never mind.

EMILY: You know, Miss Whitton, I have to tell you how much I...admire you.

CHARLOTTE: Yes, you've mentioned. Thank you.

EMILY: Do you take anything with it?

CHARLOTTE: Just clear. But ensure that the water is really boiling, not just warm.

EMILY: Of course.

CHARLOTTE: I can't abide warm tea.

EMILY: I love that you can just come out and say things like that.

CHARLOTTE: Like what?

EMILY: Well, about how you like the tea. Everyone is always so polite where I come from. Nobody would ever just come out and say what they wanted.

CHARLOTTE: A lot of warm tea drinkers. Blech.

EMILY: Yeah. Blech! What a great word! *(Pause.)* I did something yesterday that I'd never have dared to do in the eight years since I left Roger. I told him that I loved him. I was horrible to him when I broke things off and I think he's spent all this time thinking that I left because I didn't want him—that I was ashamed of him. It was in a letter, yes, and he may never read it, but for me it was like a huge burden of guilt was lifted off my shoulders. Those things that you said to me yesterday...well you're right about some of them. Maybe I would be better off in the country surrounded by a houseful of children. I know—blech! But maybe I'd love it.

CHARLOTTE: You might want to check it now.

EMILY: Oh, yes, sorry. I'm babbling.

CHARLOTTE: Don't burn yourself.

EMILY: *(She burns herself.)* Ouch!

CHARLOTTE: Let me do it. Take this. *(She hands her the bucket.)* Soak your hand in it. And for the love of God, please sit down.

EMILY sits with her hand soaking in the bucket.

EMILY: You know it's all very well to give your life to your career, but... What if you find yourself...less than what you'd hoped?

CHARLOTTE: You must have done something right to work for *Time* magazine.

EMILY: Oh, well, yes. I just can't imagine the look on Roger's face when he gets my letter.

CHARLOTTE: You're sending it?

EMILY: Don't you think I should?

CHARLOTTE: Do what you like. Just don't count on Rodney having waited eight years for your return.

EMILY: Roger. Of course I wasn't expecting him to...no, that's not true. I was hoping perhaps that the clocks had all stopped since I left and he'd be there when I was ready for him, but I suppose he isn't. Miss Whitton? Tell me it's worth it. Please.

CHARLOTTE: What does it matter what I say? If I told you to go jump off a cliff, would you do it?

EMILY: Well, no. I don't think so. Maybe.

CHARLOTTE: Is this discussion absolutely relevant to the profile?

EMILY: The profile? Oh, well no...I thought we were just talking now.

CHARLOTTE: You seem to be overly interested in personal matters and I would prefer it if we changed the subject.

EMILY: Oh. I'm sorry. All right.

EMILY hands CHARLOTTE a magazine and she looks at it.

CHARLOTTE: Where did you get this?

EMILY: I came across it when I was looking for the bucket.

CHARLOTTE: *New Liberty*. Ha.

EMILY: *New Liberty* magazine was Bill King's publication wasn't it?

CHARLOTTE: Mm.

EMILY: So you did keep in touch? This article was written by you.

CHARLOTTE: Surely you remember the story. *Time* magazine made a big to do about it. It was quite a scandal.

EMILY: Well...I've only been with *Time* a short while.

CHARLOTTE: It concerns the adoption practices in the province of Alberta. I had made a horrific discovery while conducting an internal review of the department and I felt the public had a right to know. *(She hands back the magazine.)* That article changed my life, in fact. In more ways than one.

BILL enters. Edmonton, 1946.

BILL: *(Looking out the window.)* Bless my socks. Would you look at that!

CHARLOTTE: *(Fiddling with the typewriter.)* Look at what?

BILL: How flat the land is here in Edmonton. I can see how these great stretches get the prairie dweller. "It leads on and on to that place we can never reach, but for which we always yearn."

CHARLOTTE: I wrote that.

BILL: I know.

CHARLOTTE: Blast that confounded thing! How I hate those writing machines and shall forever!

BILL: What's wrong with it this time?

CHARLOTTE: The...thingy won't budge. That huddled paragraph is due to the fact that I have just paid Acme Supplies $11.00 to have this thing overhauled and that is how it works on a first try at an automatic shift! I wish Margaret were here, she understands these things better than I.

BILL: Try using a pen. You can save the typewriter for self-defence when this article finally gets published.

CHARLOTTE: Ha ha. *(She fiddles with it a bit more.)* How dare Margaret get sick! She always does all the typing.

BILL: It's not going to be taken lightly, this.

CHARLOTTE: Good.

BILL: You've pulled the bandages off a long-festering wound, Charlotte. And with passages from your study to back it up—everyone in the country will be reading about it!

CHARLOTTE: I can't quite get used to the fact that you are my publisher. You were such a simp in college.

BILL: Don't hold back, Charlotte—what did you really think?

CHARLOTTE: It was my attempt at a compliment.

BILL: Hey! I did quite a lot of arguing in my university days, if you recall. Didn't win my biggest case, though. It's hard to compete with Canada.

CHARLOTTE: Well. Since you're so smart, why don't you do the typing and I'll dictate it to you?

BILL: Certainly. I think I make a very attractive secretary, don't you?

CHARLOTTE: A bit hairy. Ready, Mr. King?

BILL: Yes Miss Whitton.

CHARLOTTE: One of the blackest and ugliest chapters in the development of modern governments has been written against the Province of Alberta—

BILL: Good opening.

CHARLOTTE: It is a province where the Child Welfare Commission held and exercised powers without compare in any country except that of Hitler's Germany.

BILL: Hitler. That'll get their attention.

CHARLOTTE: An unparalleled story of government trafficking in illegitimate babies, exporting them to foreign homes. A story of child labour and exploitation at the hands of our own government. Dr. Whitton interviewed mothers pressured into giving up their babies—sometimes before they even saw them—

BILL: You didn't tell me that.

CHARLOTTE: And now in quotes, "Yesterday afternoon I was

> over to see a poor woman, who told me the most disturbing tale of her baby being taken from her."

BILL: Will she let us use her name?

CHARLOTTE: Secretaries don't interrupt.

BILL: No, but publishers do. It would really strengthen the piece to have a name.

CHARLOTTE: She only agreed to speak with me under the condition that she remain anonymous.

BILL: Surely you can talk her into it, with your Whittonesque powers of persuasion?

CHARLOTTE: If you had seen the poor woman, Bill. The agency coerced her in to giving it up without any options. They practically forced the pen into her hand and child out of her arms.

BILL: So she did sign something. It's legal.

CHARLOTTE: It's criminal! And what's more, there is no documentation as to where the child was placed. Which is very suspect.

BILL: You've got to get her to trust you. Force her to think of the bigger picture—that it's for the greater good of the nation. Make her feel as if her sacrifice contributed to some kind of change.

CHARLOTTE: All she wants is her baby, she doesn't care a fig about future legislation.

BILL: You mean she's a nice, *normal* woman.

CHARLOTTE: I'm going to pretend I didn't hear that.

BILL: What's the matter, Charlotte? You've not been yourself since they let you go at the Council.

CHARLOTTE: They didn't *let me go*. They were reorganizing.

BILL: This article is going to hit big. Bigger than I think you realize. Not everyone has the spine for this kind of thing. If you've gone all sentimental on me, tell me now and we'll scrap the whole idea. You can wait like a nice, well-mannered *lady*, until your survey gets lost behind years of shuffling and government hoo-hah. Is that what you want?

CHARLOTTE: Of course not.

BILL: I don't think you are in a position right now to ignore my advice.

CHARLOTTE: Which is?

BILL: Get the woman's name.

CHARLOTTE: How would you suggest I do that exactly?

BILL: I'm sure you'll think of something. Why don't you try and get her baby back? That seems to be important for some women.

She smacks him.

BILL: Oww! Now that's my girl!

BILL: You know this thing could go on for weeks yet.

CHARLOTTE: Not really!

BILL: Maybe even months if I play my cards right. Oh, don't look so horrified. I'm not such a bad fellow to spend great heaps of time with, really. And anyway, it looks as though you need someone to get you mad once in a while. I've never seen you like this before.

CHARLOTTE: Margaret is really not well Bill and If I don't make some money soon, I'm afraid I'll lose everything, including my cottage. I just hate being these thousands of miles away…

BILL: This will put your name back in the headlines,

Charlotte, and revitalize your career! I'm willing to stand behind you, no matter where this might lead, you know that. You're not alone.

CHARLOTTE: I know.

BILL: If either one of you had gotten married, you wouldn't be having these money troubles today. Sorry. It's good for my ego, though, knowing you never met anyone else. Anyway, money is the last thing I want you to be worrying about. I'll take care of anything you need until you get back on your feet.

CHARLOTTE: I can't ask you to do that.

BILL: You didn't. I offer it willingly.

CHARLOTTE: Why don't you come out to the cottage with us? We're going to need a little break anyway and then perhaps we could work out there for a while.

BILL: Why don't you just admit it, Charlotte?

Pause.

CHARLOTTE: What? Admit what?

BILL: That the two of you need a man out there to take care of things!

BILL runs off to avoid being smacked again.

EMILY: And what happened to the girl? Did she agree to have her name used?

CHARLOTTE: Yes.

EMILY: Did she ever get her baby back?

CHARLOTTE: I don't know. I didn't correspond with her after the article was published.

EMILY: Really? Not even a letter?

CHARLOTTE: Perhaps I should have written to her. Other things happened.

EMILY: What other things? Did you even try to get her baby back?

CHARLOTTE: I'm a policy maker, not a social worker.

EMILY: You lied to her?

CHARLOTTE: I needed it for the article. You can't get all weepy over every little sob story in this field; otherwise you'll be accused of being weak and womanly. I'm sorry, that's how it is. I didn't invent the rules.

EMILY: But you promised her—

CHARLOTTE: Only to reveal the truth.

EMILY: For the greater good of the nation.

CHARLOTTE: Yes.

EMILY: What about Bill?

CHARLOTTE: What about him?

EMILY: Did he keep *his* promise?

CHARLOTTE: His promise?

EMILY: To stick by you, no matter what happened. So you wouldn't be alone.

MARGARET: *(Entering with a newspaper.)* Well, it's in the newspaper again today. I suppose that means it's really happening.

EMILY: He stayed in love with you, didn't he?

CHARLOTTE: Believe me, it wouldn't have worked out.

MARGARET: I don't want you to leave now, darling, just when I'm beginning to feel a little better. If you go to jail, how will I see you? Do I slip a file in a baked good or something? It sounds a little bit exciting actually.

EMILY: But why wouldn't it? Sorry, but it doesn't make sense. He waited for you for so long, he understood and supported your work. Surely by this time he wasn't looking to have any children.

MARGARET: *(Reading.)* "Dr. Charlotte Whitton and Mr. Bill King of *New Liberty* Magazine to Stand Trial for Publishing Defamatory Libel against the Province of Alberta." Which picture did they use? Not the frowny one, I hope. Oh, good. You're smiling in this one. That's lovely. It looks as if you don't mind being sued for libel in the least. That's a good image to project, I think. You're so beautiful.

EMILY: Miss Whitton, I've been on my own for my whole adult life and I don't claim to know how your celibacy has worked for you, but I'm tired of it. I've denied myself so much that love has become an obsession with me.

CHARLOTTE: That's blindingly apparent!

EMILY: How do you do it? How do you live without love?

CHARLOTTE: Go back and marry your bumpkin then! No one's stopping you.

EMILY: You are! I want to know your secret.

CHARLOTTE: My secret?

EMILY: Yes. How did you do it? How did you stay strong?

CHARLOTTE: I was in love with someone else! Are you so thick that you haven't figured that out?

Pause.

EMILY: You had a lover?

Pause.

CHARLOTTE: I'm going to have to go back out to Edmonton and rally some more support. I might be gone for a lot longer this time.

MARGARET: Do what you have to do.

CHARLOTTE: I hate to leave you again so soon darling, but I will write every day I promise.

MARGARET: The people need you more than I.

CHARLOTTE: It's for the good of the people that I do everything, Margaret.

MARGARET: Oh, I do know that, darling. I only hope "the people" will appreciate and love you like I do someday.

CHARLOTTE: Sometimes I think I'm always disappointing you.

MARGARET: It's just guilt. Whenever a person feels guilty, it's because their conscience is talking to them.

CHARLOTTE: My conscience is screaming!

MARGARET: Tell me, are you ashamed of me?

CHARLOTTE: I…why should I be ashamed?

MARGARET: You know why.

CHARLOTTE: It's my work…

MARGARET: It won't matter to God how much you worked or how successful you were in your life.

CHARLOTTE: It matters to me! I refuse to leave this earth in anonymity. It only matters what I accomplish and the legacy that I leave behind!

MARGARET: Listen to what you're saying!

CHARLOTTE: I will make a name for myself before I die! I'll not be brushed aside when I'm old like useless dust!

MARGARET: Is that what you think? That all the rest of us who lead private, modest lives—are useless dust?

CHARLOTTE: No, no, you misunderstand.

MARGARET: I'm not changing the world. I'm living in it. It doesn't matter to anyone what I leave behind. I just want peace and our normal lives together. But I know that it's important to you what people think so I'm giving you these.

MARGARET hands CHARLOTTE a tin box.

CHARLOTTE: My letters? Darling, these are my letters to you. Surely you want to keep them?

MARGARET: I finally got to use the lighter you gave me.

CHARLOTTE: *(Waits for more, then something dawns on her. She opens the tin and gasps. She reaches in and touches the contents—ashes.)* Margaret. Margaret! How could you?

MARGARET: I don't fit in to the legacy that you want so badly to leave behind.

CHARLOTTE: I poured my heart out to you in those letters!

MARGARET: And I still have them. *(Indicating her head.)* In here.

CHARLOTTE: But you'll forget! You'll get old and forget!

MARGARET: Or die.

CHARLOTTE: You had no right to burn my letters!

MARGARET: I assumed, since they were addressed to me, that they were my letters.

CHARLOTTE: But burning them, Margaret! They're…artifacts!

MARGARET: I don't want artifacts! I want you!

CHARLOTTE: I can't just abandon this cause. The whole point of publishing the article in the first place was to draw attention to the matter. I've scheduled speaking engagements, rallies, interviews. I couldn't stay home now even if I wanted to!

MARGARET: So you don't want to.

CHARLOTTE: That's not what I'm saying! Oh. Margaret sometimes you are so...

MARGARET: Say it!

CHARLOTTE: Selfish!

MARGARET: And you're not!

CHARLOTTE: Of course I want to stay with you! Of course I do! I'm doing this for the future of Canadian children. This is so much bigger than us! I need to find them some peace!

Pause.

MARGARET: How can we find some peace?

CHARLOTTE: Perhaps we cannot.

MARGARET: I see.

CHARLOTTE: I don't know what else I can say right now.

MARGARET: I never wanted to be a wife and here I am acting like one.

CHARLOTTE: What do you want me to do?

MARGARET: I want you to go to Alberta, stand up and intimidate every last one of those dastardly politicians!

CHARLOTTE: Why don't you come with me?

MARGARET: You know I can't. My place is here. And who would look after me? I want to avoid going back to the hospital for as long as possible.

CHARLOTTE: You are not going back to the hospital. I'm going to win my case. And after, I'll plan to take some time off and we can spend every day together.

MARGARET: I would like that.

Pause.

CHARLOTTE: Do you have any poems for me this time or did you burn those too?

MARGARET: No. I do have one.

CHARLOTTE: All right, let's hear it!

MARGARET: I knew you'd be mad about the letters, so I tried to put some humour into it.

CHARLOTTE: Fantastic!

MARGARET: But I don't think it's very funny.

CHARLOTTE: I'll be the judge of that. Go on.

MARGARET: Okay, here it goes.

> Darling, we are growing old
> Silver threads among the gold
> Food gives cramps and feet grow cold
> Chins drop down and tummies fold
> Teeth drop out and age is told
> By bones that creak and wrinkles bold

CHARLOTTE: You'll let me know, Margaret, when the hilarious bit comes?

MARGARET: No, no, wait, it gets better!

> When to all the secret's sold,
> Will you love me when I'm old?
> The girls we were remain the same
> When bodies lose their youthful frame.
> So when we're locked in passion's kiss

> You really must remember this.
> Between our mouths our gums are bare
> But joined we have one tooth to share.

MARGARET: That's the end. That's the punch line.

CHARLOTTE: Oh hello, you.

MARGARET: Do you like it?

CHARLOTTE: What would I do without you, Miss?

MARGARET: You put up the tea. I'll get the biscuits.

> *She exits. BILL comes in with the newspaper and throws it on to CHARLOTTE's desk.*

BILL: Did you see it? We got *the* headline in the evening edition and Ghandi's assassination attempt the second! And in smaller print! Ghandi! Whose death may mean the violent eruption of all of Asia!

CHARLOTTE: Typical of our decadent day and this immature province!

BILL: Stop being so gloomy—the press is on our side! You were a powerhouse today. That little slip of a magistrate—I thought he was going to quiver away into a heap of nerves! Those men can hardly look you in the eyes! *Time* magazine is calling you "Canada's Joan of Arc."

CHARLOTTE: So I'm to be burned at the stake on top of everything else.

BILL: What's the matter with you?

CHARLOTTE: Why are we stuck here?! And on Thanksgiving of all weeks!

BILL: You know why. It's very important that we be in this province for the public support.

CHARLOTTE: You got me in to this whole mess and I'm failing!

BILL: It's politics. It's messy! And since when have you ever failed at anything in your life?

CHARLOTTE: What if this is the first time?

BILL: I know it's frightening, but this trial is very important, whether we win or not. And you don't have to worry, we're in this thing together.

CHARLOTTE: I just want to get away from all of this and go home!

BILL: I know it's hard to be away from home…

CHARLOTTE: What do you know about home?

BILL: I beg your pardon?

CHARLOTTE: Tell me what you know about home. What it's like to have someone there waiting for you every night? Someone who sacrifices everything so that you can traipse around the country doing God knows what? Someone to cheer you and celebrate when you bring home your hard-earned trophies? What do you know about that?

BILL: I know nothing of those things Charlotte.

CHARLOTTE: You are a selfish man! Thinking only of your article and nothing else—so you can raise the profile of your magazine and your name! At my expense!

BILL: That's just not true! If we go to jail, I lose *New Liberty*, a magazine that I've spent decades building up. I risked everything for this. For you.

CHARLOTTE: For me? Hah! No one would risk their entire career for another person. You'd have to be daft and a fool to boot! Wasting your life like that. Selfish!

BILL: Since when did love become a selfish pursuit? I've gladly given to you, Charlotte. For almost thirty years now, I've been your friend and I've occasionally asked for the odd thing—your hand in marriage for one, but don't ever try and suggest that I've wasted my life! I've withstood a lot from you. Do you think it's been easy being your friend? Perhaps I am a daft fool, but to call me selfish, that's one thing I will not accept!

CHARLOTTE: Then don't accept it! Stand up for yourself for once in your life!

Silence.

BILL: You can do what you like until the trial begins. Go home for Thanksgiving if that's what will make you happy. I'll clear my things out of this office and we needn't have any more personal contact other than discussions with our lawyers about the case. When the trial is over, don't count on my support. As of this minute consider my friendship with you withdrawn. Selfish enough for you?

Pause.

CHARLOTTE: Not bad.

BILL: The thing about being truly selfish, Charlotte, is that you can't recognize the best things in your life until they're gone. *(He exits.)*

MARGARET enters. Thanksgiving, McGregor Lake.

MARGARET: *(Off.)* Charlotte?

CHARLOTTE: Is that you? Mardie? I have your tea here, luv.

MARGARET: *(Entering—CHARLOTTE helps her to sit.)* Oh. That's lovely. Hello.

CHARLOTTE: I have to consult with you about that damned bird. I can't for the life of me figure out which end to stuff it.

MARGARET: You really shouldn't go to all the trouble, dear.

CHARLOTTE: Nonsense. It's Thanksgiving and on Thanksgiving we have a turkey. We have always had a turkey and there is no reason to forfeit tradition due to illness. Traditions are what keep us rooted to this earth.

MARGARET: I'm afraid I haven't much of an appetite Sharlie.

CHARLOTTE: You will humour me by taking a little something though won't you dear? I am going to a lot of trouble to make things the same.

MARGARET: And I appreciate that Darling. You look so sweet in my apron—all fluttering about—but I really don't know who will eat it all. It seems a shame for you to go to all the work.

CHARLOTTE: I would have invited Penelope and Nell but you told me you weren't up for company—

MARGARET: —and indeed I'm not—

CHARLOTTE: —well then, I trust that you will kindly inform me as to which end our dear fowl will receive her comeuppance?!

MARGARET: I am sorry I can't help you in the kitchen, if that's what this is about.

CHARLOTTE: Oh hush, you have always prepared the feast and I certainly can't complain about fixing it this one time, but believe me—you can have your job back next year when you're better.

MARGARET: *(Softly.)* I won't be here next year, my love.

>   *CHARLOTTE exits. MARGARET looks at the tea. She tries to pour herself a cup, but she can't lift the pot. She accidentally knocks the teacup to the floor, smashing it.*

CHARLOTTE: *(Entering with parsnips.)* Margaret! For heaven's sake. Don't try to do this on your own! I can take care of it. Oh, look at this mess. That was mother's china. Oh!

She picks up the pieces of the broken cup.

MARGARET looks at the parsnips which CHARLOTTE put into her lap during the exchange. CHARLOTTE picks up the pieces of the broken cup.

MARGARET: I'm terribly sorry, luv.

CHARLOTTE: About what, dear heart?

MARGARET: I'm sorry about your mother's cup. That was truly a shame.

CHARLOTTE: Don't be ridiculous. I should never have brought it out. *(Silence—CHARLOTTE cleaning.)*

MARGARET: Hello. *(She holds up the parsnips like bunny ears.)* Hello, Charl. *(Makes bunny noises.)*

CHARLOTTE: What are you doing with those parsnips? Margaret. I'm perfectly capable of putting up the dinner. You seem to be mocking me and I'm not happy about it. I'm not happy about it at all. *(She starts to cry.)*

MARGARET: Charl, we've had thirty such good years, let's not spoil them now.

CHARLOTTE: You know I would stay if I could!

MARGARET: Of course you would. Here, take this. *(She hands her a note.)* Keep if for the trial and know that I'm with you no matter what.

CHARLOTTE: I'll come home just as soon as it's over. And we'll celebrate together.

MARGARET: I would like that.

CHARLOTTE: You can count on it.

MARGARET: Now, why don't you dry your tears, go into the kitchen, bring me the bird and the dressing and the trusses and we'll prepare it right here in the sitting room. *(Pause.)* Hello.

CHARLOTTE: Hello.

The Supreme Court of Alberta—Edmonton, Nov. 1947

MAGISTRATE's
VOICE: The Crown vs. Charlotte Whitton and William King. All rise. Firstly, the said Charlotte Whitton between the 1st day of April 1946, and the 30th day of July, 1947, did unlawfully conspire, combine, confederate, and agree to commit an indictable offence contrary to section 573 of the Criminal Code of Canada, such offense being to publish a defamatory libel concerning the Child Welfare Commission of the Province of Alberta and the members thereof...

CHARLOTTE: Margaret, are you there? Margaret! I have your note tucked in my sleeve that you tried so desperately to write; you wrote, "I know you will come out all right." It's not I, darling. It's these children and the aged and ill and for all time to come for the future and for the future of all their children in turn. Please, don't go! Not yet! Just hang on for a while longer and I'll be able to be by your side. I hold your ring so that I can feel you with me. I'm so afraid, but not for the reasons they think. I can't show them my fear, I can't cry in case it is construed as weakness.

MARGARET: Oh my, Charlotte. I only wish that I could have held on.

CHARLOTTE: Margaret?

She turns to look at her.

MARGARET: I'm here. I'm right here, luv.

CHARLOTTE: Oh Margaret, even on your deathbed, I asked for your strength for my self—I held on to your letter so tightly thinking that I could prevent your passing—that I could somehow will you to stay. And I swear I heard your voice in my ear at the moment of your death. You said…

MARGARET: …It won't be that way, not now, not for a while.

CHARLOTTE: And it suddenly struck me that all that time, I should have been fighting for you.

MARGARET: Hello. *(She exits.)*

EMILY: Margaret.

CHARLOTTE: Margaret Jean Grier.

EMILY: You were in love with a woman?

CHARLOTTE: Yes. I…loved her. She meant everything in the world to me but I spent so much time with my selfish pursuits that I neglected her and let her die on her own. And after all that, they dropped the charges against me.

EMILY: So all the lectures? The papers you've given about sacrifice! They're lies?

CHARLOTTE: Not lies. I was ashamed. But it was never Margaret I was ashamed of, and I didn't get to tell her that. I simply never wanted to admit that I needed someone.

EMILY: Even you.

CHARLOTTE: *(She finds her book and gives it to EMILY.)* Here! Take it! I want you to read it—all of it!

EMILY: *(Reading the front cover.)* Molly Mugwump Makes Believe.

CHARLOTTE: A Mugwump is a very small troll who sits on a fence unable to move forward or back. Molly is me. The Make-Believe is Margaret, because I talk to her as if she's still alive.

EMILY: These are all letters you wrote to her *after* she died?

CHARLOTTE: Every day for nearly three years. I just kept on as we've always done—reporting the details of my day, sharing my thoughts. I even clipped out articles for her.

EMILY looks through the book.

EMILY: Did Bill ever know?

CHARLOTTE: I don't know. If he did, he never let on. The last time I saw him was at Margaret's funeral, but he kept his word. We never spoke again. One thing about Bill, he was always a man of his word. All I have of them both are my memories, but memories don't stay. The photos and the letters are like strings on a finger—they just remind you that there's something you must have forgotten.

EMILY: *(Takes her letter to Roger out of her pocket.)*

CHARLOTTE: What's that?

EMILY: My letter to Roger. No offence, but I don't want it to turn into a book.

She throws her letter in to the stove and watches it burn.

CHARLOTTE: Oh, just burn mine as well. I've told you most of it anyway.

EMILY: I can't burn these letters!

CHARLOTTE: Well, go ahead! Publish the damn things then. I've been hiding them for so long, it will be a relief! Who knows? You may even win *Time*'s Journalist of the Year!

EMILY: Oh, but that's not why...

CHARLOTTE: And I will go down in history as serving the shortest mayoral term in Canada. That will be my legacy. Finally.

EMILY: Miss Whitton—

CHARLOTTE: Go on! Do it. I'd probably do the same if I were you.

EMILY: —I don't even write for *Time*.

Pause.

EMILY: I write for a small weekly. In fashion.

Pause.

EMILY: I lied to you. I lied so that I could have a chance to meet you. But that's not why I can't burn your letters. You have to do it. *(She goes to CHARLOTTE and puts the book in her hand.)* You have to burn your own letters.

CHARLOTTE: *(She holds the book over the stove.)* I can't. If I burn it, how will people know about her after I'm gone?

EMILY: Is that what you want?

Pause.

CHARLOTTE: I let Margaret be forgotten in life. I don't want to do the same in her death.

EMILY: Well, why don't you just let the make-believe part come to an end? I don't think you have to burn the letters to do that.

CHARLOTTE: But what's to become of them? The world is not yet capable of accepting a union such as ours. They'd turn it into something vulgar. I couldn't bear that.

EMILY: Why don't you seal them up in a vault somewhere until people are ready to understand. In ten, twenty years.

CHARLOTTE: The next century perhaps.

EMILY: You're the first lady mayor in Canada, Miss Whitton. Imagine everyone's surprise fifty years from now, when they see that you had a first lady too!

CHARLOTTE: I would like to see that.

Pause.

EMILY: Now, why don't you close up the lid and we'll have some tea.

CHARLOTTE: *(Burns herself on the handle of the lid.)* Ouch!

EMILY: Here. Sit.

Hands her the bucket of water. CHARLOTTE puts her hand in and sits. EMILY puts the kettle on the stove.

Pause. They wait for the water to boil.

CHARLOTTE: Fashion?

EMILY: Yes.

CHARLOTTE: You don't write for *Time*?

EMILY: No. I write about clothes and hats.

CHARLOTTE: That sounds very interesting.

EMILY: It does? I guess so.

CHARLOTTE: Miss Wicks, I'm having a hell of a time figuring out what to wear for the royal visit. Do you think you could…suggest something special?

EMILY: Really? Me?

CHARLOTTE: Why not?

EMILY: Um…you know I do have this design I'm working on. But no—

CHARLOTTE: What is it?

EMILY: Well…it's still in development…

CHARLOTTE: Yes?

EMILY: I don't know if you're interested in trying out the prototype…but it's very special.

CHARLOTTE: What is it for heaven's sake?

EMILY: It will transform any woman's body into a stunning work of art.

CHARLOTTE: My goodness.

EMILY: And not only that but if worn properly, your posture will be as regal as the Queen herself! I call it the Rising Sun.

CHARLOTTE: What kind of garment is it?

EMILY: It's a brassiere.

CHARLOTTE: Oh.

EMILY: But a very specially designed one—it lifts and supports the bust line without compressing the breasts.

CHARLOTTE: Aptly named.

EMILY: I've always thought there's no reason our breasts should look as though they are two torpedoes about to be launched. Would you like to try it under a three quarter sleeve suit with say…a pencil skirt? Red would be lovely on you. And you could finish it up with a cape instead of a coat. That would really look swell with white gloves and a matching handbag.

CHARLOTTE: Oh, why not?

EMILY: Really? You like the idea?

CHARLOTTE: Of course! How often does one get the chance to become a work of art?

EMILY: Wow. That's...amazing! Oh, I've got to get started right away. We'll need your measurements and cup size—

CHARLOTTE: Miss Wicks—

EMILY: Yes?

CHARLOTTE: Why don't you go for a little walk. That might calm you down until we're able to get back to the city tomorrow.

EMILY: Oh. Right. Um...do you want to come?

CHARLOTTE: Yes. You just go ahead though. I'll join you in a moment. *(EMILY goes to exit.)*

EMILY: Thanks...Charlotte.

She exits.

CHARLOTTE: Margaret. One more make-believe. I've always said, we must just keep on, we must not be defeated because time and space between us are unknown and mysterious, because we do not know when my journey's end will mean our meeting. All your life, all, I mean, of yours and mine together, we had to bridge space, the space we knew, the space that we kept only for ourselves, upheld by our letters and the hope of meeting at the journey's end. Sometimes I thought that I was writing for your sake, but now that you're gone, I realize I was really writing for myself. How I wish now that I could reclaim all of that lost space. But I suppose, Margaret, that I should finally let you rest and let the make-believe come to an end. Yesterday I made a vow to devote myself to Canada, the Queen and to the service of the people of Ottawa, and our little games might not be understood. I know that you will always be with me, and our hidden love between the pages of this diary of ours. It's a beautiful day, clear sky, warm sun, little breezes "dust and quiver." The kind of day you loved.

MARGARET appears.

Goodbye, my darling.

She goes to leave and turns back to the room.

Margaret! Before you go, did I tell you that I'm finally going to meet the future queen! And I'm gonna look swell!

CHARLOTTE
& MARGARET: Ahhhhhhh!

Blackout.

The End.

CHORUS.
Daintily.
You are my hon - ey, hon - ey - suck - le, I am the bee, ...
I'd like to sip the hon - ey sweet from those red lips, you see; ....
I love you dear - ly, dear - ly, and I want you to love me, ...
You are my hon - ey, hon - ey - suck - le, I am the bee."
Fine.

Edmonton Jan 30. 1948.

Dearest:
 Another day at its end and you and I alone together. I would not ask for other company though I would wish it were in your own green room and Ruth on the bed there! O Maudie! Maudie!
 It has been an exhausting day, dearest; that which touches me most nearly, you know, for, as I stood up in that travesty of a court room this morning, to be committed for trial, I held so tightly onto your ring and I prayed. I asked "O Margaret, closer to God, ask Him that, by the stripes which wounded you, I may be discharged." And, darling, I swear, you stood beside me close. Your arm about my shoulder, and you whispered "It won't be that way. Hot a oz, wait for awhile". I almost cried and was so fearful, it would be thought

THE MACDONALD
EDMONTON, ALBERTA
Nov. 24th.,1947.

Dear Mardie;
        Here I am up for air after three hours or more in Court and it was not very pleasant, Mr. Bruce Smith, the Government's lawyer is inclined to be unpleasant and they are going to block at every stage. Having advised weeks ago that we could have files, they this morning opposed them, etc.. etc.. But it will in the end come right. We are to be in Court every day from nine thirty to one except Friday. I think week after next I shall go down to Calgary and see Agnes as she will be able to certify that you are right there in Ottawa. I just hate this and Mr. Steer told me yesterday to get my mind on my friends in Alberta and off my friend in Ottawa.

        I had such a nice letter from Grace who says every one is being good but Rustie who is acting like a devil and saying she wants to go home. Poor Grace it is so long since she has supervised foster home placement and anyway she always favoured custodial units.

        I do so want a report from you from Hooper or some one in authority who will say when you are going to the May court and then home, James. I know those two are scheming to get you there to greet me and I want to be there and have that place all swell-differious for you*m*in my own way. I am getting two dollars a day as a fee out here so I shall have a new car for you with the 50 percent tax; Jim says he will see what Home can do for us.

        It is quite cold andd heavy snow and my overshoes haven not yet come whatever happened Murphy Gamble where I bought them over a week ago. They should have been here Thursday.

        I wrote to Rose and hope to write to the Rev. Mother tonight;We got to get you up there after Christmas if we can before you go back to the office. I told Rose to threaten Katharine with a habeas corpus on that tray if she did not have it.

        My lawyer has called for me so off I am. I am living at h' his office so much that the janitor yesterday asked me if I were Mrs. Steer. Daisy says let Cross get hold of that. He stayed in Court all morning. Love on love and do get that plumbing and sewage plant working; it is going to cost as much as the whole Ottawa filtration before we are through. Heigho Ho.

CANADA'S HOTELS OF DISTINCTION   OWNED AND OPERATED BY CANADIAN NATIONAL RAILWAYS
THE CHARLOTTETOWN, CHARLOTTETOWN . THE NOVA SCOTIAN, HALIFAX . CHATEAU LAURIER, OTTAWA . PRINCE ARTHUR HOTEL, PORT ARTHUR
THE FORT GARRY, WINNIPEG . PRINCE EDWARD HOTEL, BRANDON . THE BESSBOROUGH, SASKATOON . THE MACDONALD, EDMONTON
OPEN SUMMER SEASON ONLY: JASPER PARK LODGE, JASPER, ALTA . MINAKI LODGE, MINAKI, ONT. . PICTOU LODGE, PICTOU, N.S.
HOTEL VANCOUVER, VANCOUVER, B.C. (OPERATED UNDER THE JOINT MANAGEMENT OF THE CANADIAN NATIONAL AND CANADIAN PACIFIC RAILWAY COMPANIES)